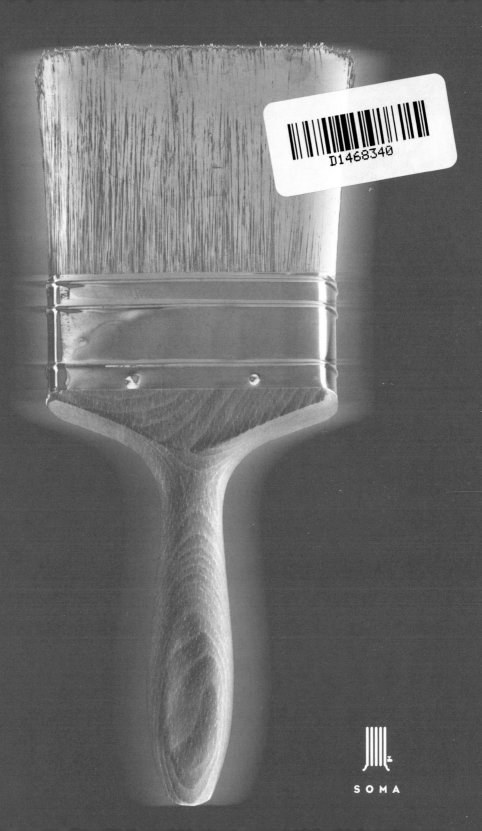

SOMA

contents

foreword

As a design writer, and as someone who has moved and decorated six times in the last four years, I continually ask myself: why does decorating have to be difficult? Whether you are planning a quick update or remodeling from scratch, there is always a great deal to consider: from getting the basics right, through planning and decorating each space, to accessorizing the look. Once you manage to make these decisions, there are almost always problems that force you to alter your plans, or compromises that have to be made before you can proceed to the next stage. As if this weren't enough, you have to sift through the staggering number of decorative looks available. No wonder many people simply give up, or call in the professionals.

I have learned from experience that the only way to keep your sanity (and bank balance) more or less intact is to be organized and methodical. In the beginning, I used to note down ideas on the first piece of paper I came across and foolishly imagined that I could memorize colors. But I soon got tired of walking around with pockets full of scrap paper, crumpled-up pieces of fabric, and dog-eared paint chips.

My experiences have evolved over time into the contents for *The Decorator's Fact File*. There is a real need for a handy-sized design guide that not only gives you lots of great ideas, but also somewhere to collect and record your thoughts and your home's vital statistics, so that this information is always easy to find. It also gives you the opportunity to write down all the jobs to be done in each room, so that you can have the satisfaction of checking them off one by one.

The Decorator's Fact File has been designed and written to help you build up a complete picture of your home. As well as showing you how to make a detailed assessment of every part of it and providing you with space to organize this information, it shows you how to divide the design process into a logical sequence, so there is much less chance of forgetting a vital element or of doing jobs in the wrong order.

Try to get into the habit of using the "home fact file" pages to record measurements, numbers and other useful information, and take it with you on shopping trips – you'll find it comes in very handy when you have to work out whether that bargain sofa is the right size, or if you've bought enough material.

One of the things I love most about this fact file is that it's packed with fast and effective ideas for smartening up and personalizing your space. In fact, there's a whole chapter devoted to the subject. I wish I had thought of some of the ideas included here a few years ago, when I found myself living in a succession of short-term rentals. Many of the traditional ways of making a new place feel like home, such as redecorating or remodeling, were simply not an option in these places. In addition, the existing decor and furnishings were sometimes less than gorgeous, so I had to think of ways to cover them up or play them down, without compromising on comfort or leaving any permanent marks.

I have suggested ways to tackle a variety of typical decorating tasks, and what each of the "home fact file" sections might be used for, but you don't have to stick to these like glue. The idea is not to mimic the ideas and methods included, but to use them as a starting point for your own ideas. In fact, I'd love to know how you have adapted this fact file to suit your needs. Just drop me a line in care of Conran Octopus, 37 Shelton Street, London WC2H 9HN, UK.

Happy decorating!

5

how to use this fact file

The *Decorator's Fact File* is unlike any other decorating book, and knowing how it works will enable you to get the most out of it. Illustrated here are the five page types that you will come across. Each of these is designed to work with the others, through cross-referencing, so that you will be able to explore a range of options, firm up your ideas, translate them into a work plan, and, finally, see it all put in to practice in beautiful finished rooms.

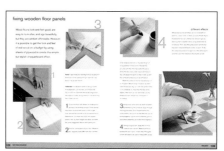

❶ strategy pages provide introductions to each decorating topic, identifying the approaches you can take, explaining how you should assess and record your needs, and directing you so that you can undertake work with confidence.

❷ directory pages set out the many choices available when considering methods and materials, from the best ways to clean a range of surfaces to the most attractive finishes available for decorating floors or walls.

❸ project pages offer professional hand-holding and step-by-step photography to take you through the essential preparatory decorating tasks and then on to the practicalities of realizing exciting creative solutions.

❹ key ingredients pages identify the building blocks of successful style – whether you are looking for stylish, reliable surface materials, ways to combine a living room with a work space, or quick fixes to give a place a summertime feel.

❺ home fact file pages are interactive pages, allowing you to fill in and build up your own personal decorating fact file. They provide somewhere for you to plan your changes and record measurements, inspiration, and decisions. You may like to photocopy blank "planning," "product choices," and other home fact file spreads to use when preparing any additional rooms for decorating, such as attics or basements.

▸ **a zip-up plastic pocket** is provided at the back of the fact file for storing inspirational decorating ideas – torn from magazines, collected as postcards or photos, or given to you as paint swatches and fabric samples.

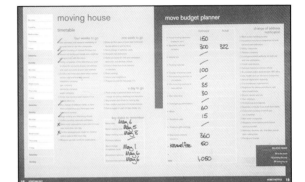

general fact file pages keep you on track.

▸ places to summarize information and costs
▸ checklists of important tasks

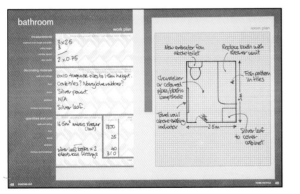

"planning" fact file pages provide easy recall of your room dimensions and your plans for change.

▸ space in which to
    record measurements
    list jobs to be done and materials needed
    keep financial records
▸ grids on which to draw room plans

"product choices" fact file pages provide instant visual recall of your color, fabric, and other decorating decisions.

▸ boxes in which to stick swatches and note the sources of your chosen decorating materials

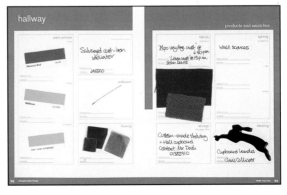

starting out

on the move

❶ When finalizing the date for your move, consider whether it might be desirable to spread it over two days (a necessity if your new home is some distance away), and don't automatically opt for a Friday (the most popular day). If possible, arrange to move midweek, so that there is a working day after the move in which to deal with any unexpected problems.

▽

Work out a budget for the move (using the planner on page 19).

▽

Decide whether you are going to do the packing and move yourself, or hire a moving company (the latter costs more, but can be worth the expense if you have little spare time or energy or have a lot of possessions to move).

▽

above **It is wise to set up a place for displaying and storing your belongings before unpacking. Makeshift but unsatisfactory storage solutions can all too easily become a fixture.**

The effort required to move should not be underestimated, but there are ways to keep the wear and tear on you, your loved ones, and your finances at a manageable level. The trick is to begin the process well ahead of the move itself.

A checklist of jobs to consider before your move is given on page 18. Use this and the following memory joggers to create your own countdown timetable.

Call your local truck rental or moving company to check their availability and costs. Make sure they understand your needs, and discuss any items that need special handling. Let them know if parking near your new home is likely to be a problem.

❷ Notify essential contacts and friends of your forthcoming change of address and move date. (See the checklist on page 19.)

one week before

❶ Give yourself plenty of time to sort and pack your belongings. Deciding whether to throw something away, or otherwise dispose of it, also takes time.

▽

Collect more packing materials than you think you will need, and don't just go for the largest boxes you can find – they will be impossible to lift when filled with heavy items. Smaller cartons are easier to carry; they can be held closer to the body, which puts less strain on the arms, back, and shoulders.

❷ It helps enormously to have made a rough plan of your new home before moving. Mark furniture and boxes with a code for each room, using colored or numbered stickers. Write these, correspondingly, on your plan, and pin it in a prominent place near the front door when unloading. Record the contents and numbers of each box in the "packing organizer" summary grid on pages 20–21.

▽

Be sure to check that your new home's doorways, windows, and/or elevators are large enough to take the sofa and other large items of furniture.

the day before

❶ Collect the items for your "survival kit" in a box, and keep this separate from the rest of your packing.

▽

Try to go to bed early.

moving day

❶ Begin the day with a good breakfast. The next decent meal will probably be several hours away.

▽

If it is a rainy day, it is a good idea to protect the entrance hall floor with drop cloths, and remember to take them with you for use at the other end.

❷ Before loading up, explain your labeling system to helpers or the moving company staff, and indicate which items you plan to carry personally.

❸ Once all the loading has been done, make a final check of the rooms (and built-in cupboards) to ensure that nothing has been left behind.

▽

Leave the keys, with labels attached indicating their use, with the real estate agent or building manager for use by the next occupant.

arriving at your new home

❶ Put the heavier items of furniture into place. Check that you have hot water and electricity. Make the beds and, if necessary, hang bedroom curtains or blinds. Unpack your survival kit only – the place will look tidier, you will be less exhausted, and it will be easier to give cupboards and shelves a good cleaning.

▽

Take some time to stop and relax.

survival kit

- ▸ Coffeemaker and/or tea kettle.
- ▸ Tea, coffee, and water.
- ▸ Sugar.
- ▸ Disposable/unbreakable cups and plates.
- ▸ Cutlery, corkscrew and can opener.
- ▸ Soap, multi surface cleaner, and bleach.
- ▸ Sponges and cloths.
- ▸ Bedding and towels.
- ▸ Soap, shampoo, and medications.
- ▸ Toilet paper.
- ▸ First aid kit.
- ▸ Contact details (see list on page 24).
- ▸ Cash, checkbook, and credit cards.
- ▸ A change of clothes, plus pajamas and slippers.
- ▸ Flashlight.
- ▸ Extension cord.
- ▸ Basic tool kit (see pages 56–57).
- ▸ Contract with moving company or truck rental company.
- ▸ Driver's license.
- ▸ A bottle of your favorite celebratory beverage.

RELATED PAGES

18 home fact file: moving

20 packing organizer

56 tool kit

packing

Whether you regard packing as a thrill or a chore, it pays to give your possessions some care and attention when you are moving. Items take up less space when folded or stacked neatly in boxes (so you'll have fewer to lift and carry) and are better able to withstand the odd bump or knock. They are also easier to locate and unpack at the other end (there are few tasks more dispiriting after a move than hunting for a missing sock, or trying to find enough forks for everyone to sit down to a meal).

books: only pack a few at a time

books and magazines should only be packed in small boxes, or they will be impossible to lift.

china and glass should be individually wrapped in layers of newspaper and stacked in boxes. Place

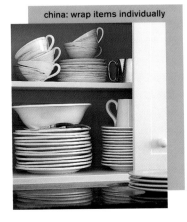

china: wrap items individually

a thick cushion of crumpled paper or towels in the base of the box, place large plates and lids vertically around the sides (they take up less space this way), and fill the center with smaller items. Make sure that the boxes are clearly labeled as fragile.

clothes and linens should be packed into suitcases and traveling bags. To save time unpacking, use "wardrobe" cartons (supplied with a clip-on rack) to transport clothes on their hangers.

foods Try not to transport fresh or perishable items. If this is unavoidable, wrap them carefully and carry them in an insulated cooler.

refrigerators, stoves, and dishwashers should be transported empty and upright. Remove

any loose shelves or baskets from the insides before moving them. Let refrigerators and freezers stand in their new home for several hours before turning them on again.

furniture should be wrapped in plastic sheeting, or blankets if highly polished. Remove any loose shelves before transportation, or dismantle completely. Tape screws or fittings to an inside surface, to avoid hunting for them later, and number loose items if they need to be fitted in a particular order.

home computers may have a "park" facility to prevent the hard disk

computer: carry it with you

from being damaged while moving – see your owner's manual for details. Their fragility and cost, and the misery of a malfunction or breakdown, means that they are best transported in a box on a car seat rather than in the truck.

kitchen equipment, including saucepans and other small unbreakables, can be wrapped in newspaper, to prevent scratching, and placed in boxes. Knives and sharp implements should be grouped, wrapped in bubble wrap and clearly marked, to prevent injury.

large breakables such as lamps, stereos, and TVs will need to be packed in suitably sized boxes filled with polystyrene packing material. Ask a local electrical or china shop if they have any spare packing materials.

musical instruments

Put smaller instruments in their carry cases and transport them personally. Pianos should be entrusted to a moving company that knows how to handle them, and then left to recover for a few weeks before being retuned.

instruments: take extra care

pets are likely to find the move stressful too. It may be better to leave them with a friend or relative for the day. When you bring them into your new home for the first time, make

pets: keep them calm

sure the doors and windows are kept shut to stop them from running off. Keep dogs on the leash during walks until they are familiar with the new area.

pictures need wrapping in corrugated cardboard to protect the edges and frames. Transport them wrapped in blankets to prevent them from rubbing against other surfaces.

rugs and carpets should be rolled (patterned surface inwards) rather than folded, to prevent creases and protect them from dirt and damage in transit.

toiletries should be packed in plenty of absorbent paper or newspaper. Stand bottles upright in boxes and mark them "This End Up."

valuables such as jewelry and important papers should be carried on you or with you (perhaps packed among some clothing), rather than in the truck.

move it safely

- Use rugs and blankets to protect polished furniture and other surfaces.
- The contents of drawers can be moved in situ, but cover them with towels to keep them from moving around. Remove drawers when loading and unloading furniture.
- Make sure that rooms and paths are clear of obstructions.
- When loading a truck, try to make flat surfaces with boxes, so that they can be stacked on top of one another.
- Before lifting an item, make sure it can be grasped firmly. Keep your back straight, and bend at the hips and knees. Straighten up gradually.
- Heavy items should be packed low down and evenly distributed.
- Damage is caused by items moving around in the truck. Wedge things firmly in place, and use ropes and tape to secure them to the sides if necessary.

what have you got?

above **A wall of windows, high ceilings, and a good wood floor make this an instantly appealing space – with the opportunity to keep furnishings very simple.**

opposite **Plenty of existing storage is a great benefit, but you may feel that cupboards such as these take up too much space and obscure the light.**

Every home has its good and bad points. Some will be easy to spot; others may only become apparent over time: sunshine will seem to bounce around the room at certain times of year, but struggle to enter at others, and a noisy radiator that you hardly noticed at first, becomes more and more annoying.

Taking a detailed look at your home should be your first step, whether you're planning to give it a fast facelift or rip everything out and start again. By assessing the whole, it will be much easier to prioritize and make the best use of your finances.

room by room assessment

The first thing you will notice about any room is its decorative condition, and getting rid of that nasty wallpaper or tired carpet will seem like a natural first step. Before you do, however, try to look beyond the surface at the structural state of the room.

walls and ceiling: Are the walls straight? Is the plaster cracked? Are there any bulges, stains, or other signs of dampness? Are there gaps where the baseboards meet the walls and floor?

floors: Do they slope? Are the floorboards (if you have them) in good condition?

doors and windows: Do they open and shut smoothly? Does the door jut awkwardly into the room when open, and make it difficult to arrange the furniture? It might be possible to solve this by rehanging the door. Is the view from the bedroom window better than that from the living room? Would you be prepared to swap rooms around?

utilities: Check that the plumbing, heating, and electricity are adequate. You may find that the outlets in your new living room are too few and awkwardly placed, or that there are signs of moisture around bathtubs and sinks. Seemingly drab rooms can be transformed by the addition of a well-placed mirror and light fixtures.

After making your assessment, note the jobs you think need to be done in each room in your "home fact file," pages 22–23.

rethinking the layout

advantages: This need not be difficult or expensive. Non-load-bearing walls can be erected or dismantled in a matter of hours – and it can pay huge dividends to do so in a small or poorly laid-out property.

disadvantages: The building's construction may well impose limitations – it's difficult, for example, to move bathrooms

very far because of all the plumbing involved, and load-bearing walls may have to stay where they are. You will also need to call in experts such as building contractors and plasterers, and be prepared for a great deal of mess and disruption.

RELATED PAGES

22 structural changes
54 renovate and repair
58 preparing walls
60 preparing woodwork

thinking about the practicalities

When assessing or designing a room, ask yourself: "does it work?" By this we don't mean "Does the faucet drip?" or "Will the key turn in the lock?" Instead, we are trying to ascertain whether the room, and every element within it, does its job properly, and whether it fits in with the rest of the design. Will it be easy to carry shopping into the kitchen, and food into the living room? How will the neutral gray paint color being considered for the hall look when viewed from the bright yellow living room?

Most of us sheepishly follow convention when it comes to assigning space to activities. The biggest room, for example, invariably becomes the living room, although there is no reason why it shouldn't be the kitchen or your office, if you could do with more space for these activities. Think about the sorts of

right **Light and movable furniture allows great flexibility in the layout of a room. Simple, elegant pieces, such as this storage cabinet, also make good choices, as they will adapt with the changes, over time, in your decorative style.**

rooms that make you feel comfortable: Do you relax by sprawling on the bed in front of the TV, or are you happier cooking and chatting to someone at the same time? If you plan to socialize or spend a reasonable amount of time in a room, it makes sense to ensure that it is up to the task.

There will be practical considerations too. Rooms that are used by more than one person at a time need to be large enough to allow each occupant to spread themselves out, while retaining a sense of personal space. Storage requirements and, of course, plumbing also play a part in determining whether a room's use can be changed.

what to do with excess belongings

Despite having thrown out sackfuls of junk before the move, you are bound to find that there simply isn't room, or the need, for some of the things that you brought with you.

things that are in good condition

▸ Have a garage sale.
▸ Sell them through the classifieds section of your local paper or through a specialist magazine.
▸ Auction houses are a good place to sell furniture and other household items. (See the auctioneers and describe what you want to sell, as most will only handle certain types of goods, or those of a certain standard.) Alternatively, contact local second-hand furniture dealers.

things that are old but too good to be thrown away

▸ Donate them to charity shops and rummage sales.
▸ Ask a friend or relative to look after them on loan.

home fact file
first steps

When moving, careful planning helps to reduce stress and confusion. These pages include a budget planner and a checklist of jobs to be done in advance; a checklist for informing people of your change of address; a guide for keeping track of your packing; space for itemizing structural changes (such as, "replace sash windows and sand down sills"); and room for essential phone and fax numbers and e-mail addresses.

moving

timetable

Monday	
Tuesday	
Wednesday	
Thursday	
Friday	
Saturday	
Sunday	
Monday	
Tuesday	
Wednesday	
Thursday	
Friday	
Saturday	
Sunday	
Monday	
Tuesday	
Wednesday	
Thursday	
Friday	
Saturday	
Sunday	

four weeks to go

☐ Get estimates and research availability of moving companies or truck rental companies.

☐ Confirm booking of moving company/truck rental.

☐ Sound out family and friends who might be willing to help with the move.

☐ Notify companies of the date that you wish to close the accounts at your old address and open accounts at your new address.

☐ Confirm the times and dates when meters will be read and final bills issued:

gas _____

electricity _____

water _____

☐ Order new furniture and carpets if you have not already done so.

☐ Buy change of address cards, or have them printed once you have your new telephone number.

☐ Begin sorting and disposing of junk.

☐ Collect packing materials and labels.

☐ Make hotel reservations if you plan to move over more than one day.

☐ Confirm arrangements made for children and/or pets on the move day.

☐ Measure new rooms for scale plans.

one week to go

☐ Draw up floor plans of your new home and decide where to put furniture.

☐ Send change of address cards.

☐ Request mail forwarding.

☐ Settle accounts for newspaper deliveries.

☐ Collect items from local cleaners.

☐ Start packing.

☐ Inform your neighbors.

☐ Prepare survival kit (see page 11).

a day to go

☐ Pack a bag of personal items such as a change of clothes, toiletries, and valuables.

☐ Buy snacks and drinks for moving day.

☐ Take children and pets to friends/relatives.

☐ Get a supply of cash for tips, meals, etc.

key dates to remember

Move date _____

Meter reading (old) _____

Meter reading (new) _____

Furniture delivery _____

Send change
of address cards _____

Disconnect utilities _____

Connect utilities _____

move budget planner

	Estimated	Actual
▶ House-hunting expenses (transport, etc.)		
▶ Moving company		
▶ Truck rental		
▶ Packing materials		
▶ Change of address cards		
▶ Reconnecting utilities at new address		
▶ Overnight accommodations		
▶ Meals		
▶ Telephone calls		
▶ Thank-you gifts and tips		
▶ Insurance for new home and its contents		
▶		
▶		
▶		
total		

change of address notification

- ☐ Bank or credit union.
- ☐ Homeowner's insurance companies for both old and new addresses.
- ☐ Utility companies.
- ☐ Post office.
- ☐ Credit card issuers.
- ☐ IRS.
- ☐ Accountant.
- ☐ Life, health, and car insurance companies.
- ☐ Motor vehicle department.
- ☐ Automobile association.
- ☐ Broker, mutual funds and other investment companies.
- ☐ Doctor, dentist, and vet.
- ☐ Your employer.
- ☐ Professional associations.
- ☐ Business contacts if you work from home.
- ☐ Clubs and societies of which you are a member.
- ☐ Mail-order companies.
- ☐ Magazine subscriptions and Internet service provider.
- ☐ Galleries, theaters, etc. that have you on their mailing lists.
- ☐ Family and friends.

RELATED PAGES

10 on the move
12 packing
36 measuring

packing organizer

Box number or code:

Destination:

Contents:

Box number or code:

Destination:

Contents:

Box number or code:

Destination:

Contents:

Box number or code:

Destination:

Contents:

Box number or code:

Destination:

Contents:

Box number or code:

Destination:

Contents:

Box number or code:

Destination:

Contents:

Box number or code:

Destination:

Contents:

Box number or code:

Destination:

Contents:

Record the contents, destination, and the box code of your packing, to enable you to trace items easily on arrival at your new home.

Box number or code:

Destination:

Contents:

Box number or code:

Destination:

Contents:

Box number or code:

Destination:

Contents:

Box number or code:

Destination:

Contents:

Box number or code:

Destination:

Contents:

Box number or code:

Destination:

Contents:

Box number or code:

Destination:

Contents:

Box number or code:

Destination:

Contents:

Box number or code:

Destination:

Contents:

structural changes

living room

changes to structure

walls

floor

ceiling

doors and windows

built-in furniture

changes to utilities

heating

lighting

electricity

communications

summary of costs

structure

utilities

total

kitchen

changes to structure

walls

floor

ceiling

doors and windows

built-in furniture

changes to utilities

heating

lighting

electricity

plumbing

cooking

summary of costs

structure

utilities

total

hall/basement/attic

changes to structure

walls

floor

ceiling

doors and windows

built-in furniture

changes to utilities

heating

lighting

electricity

plumbing

communications

summary of costs

structure

utilities

total

Use these pages to summarize the changes to be made to structure and utilities (including any preparation for decorating).

bedroom

changes to structure

walls

floor

ceiling

doors and windows

built-in furniture

changes to utilities

heating

lighting

electricity

plumbing

communications

summary of costs

structure

utilities

total

bathroom

changes to structure

walls

floor

ceiling

doors and windows

built-in furniture

changes to utilities

heating

lighting

electricity

plumbing

summary of costs

structure

utilities

total

study

changes to structure

walls

floor

ceiling

doors and windows

built-in furniture

changes to utilities

heating

lighting

electricity

communications

summary of costs

structure

utilities

total

contact numbers

	telephone	fax	e-mail
Real estate agent			
Lawyer			
Financial adviser			
Bank or credit union			
Moving company/truck			
rental company			
Move helpers			
New landlord			
Old landlord			
Previous occupant of new home			
New occupant of old home			
Electric company			
Gas company			
Water company			
Telephone company			
Contractor			
Painter/decorator			
Plumber			
Electrician			

what do you want?

There is no right or wrong way to design a room. Designers will suggest that you build a plan around a favorite object or around the floor, but if you're happier playing around with colors and furniture until the mix feels right, then that is the method you should use.

Truly successful design, however, is about creating rooms that work on a practical, as well as an aesthetic, level, and ensuring that the end result makes the best possible use of the available budget.

practical questions

▸ How long do I plan to live here?

▸ If this room is to have more than one use (an office/bedroom for example), will it give rise to conflict? If two or more people share this room, does this make the problem worse?

▸ Does the existing layout give me enough privacy? Or allow me to screen off untidy areas such as the kitchen?

▸ Does the layout give me space to entertain, work or spend time on my hobbies? Hang the wash to dry on rainy days?

▸ Do I have children or pets to consider when choosing finishes and materials?

aesthetic questions

▸ Do I share my home with someone who has similar or different tastes? Would it help to divide responsibility for decorating the rooms?

▸ Do I have strong likes and dislikes when it comes to color and pattern? If someone were to decorate my home in my absence, would I view the results with an open mind?

▸ Do I have a favorite architectural or decorative style?

▸ Are there objects or items of furniture that I simply can't live without?

budgetary questions

▸ What is the maximum I can afford to spend on changes (including emergencies)?

▸ Have I done any research into the likely costs? Contractors' estimates, for example, or the current prices for essential kitchen appliances? (If not, obtain them before splurging on that irresistible curtain fabric.)

▸ Would learning a new skill, such as tiling, ease the pressures on my budget?

▸ Will I have to borrow money to carry out even basic improvements? If so, is it worth borrowing more to get better prices on larger orders for materials and services?

above **A room with a strong sense of style. The all-white backdrop is anything but stark when warmed by substantial, boldly colored pieces such as the sofa throw and wall artwork. An eclectic mix of furniture finds harmony in unified color, to produce a highly individual and successful scheme.**

think in three dimensions

Before you start decorating or furnishing a room, it always pays to assess the shape of the space. Stand in the middle of the room and ask yourself: Does it feel awkwardly or well proportioned? Does there seem to be a lot of wasted space? (Is this perhaps because the furniture is awkwardly arranged, or because there is more than one door into the room?) Are there attractive focal points, such as windows or fireplaces, or does the room feel strangely featureless?

Getting answers to questions such as these will help you to work out how to manipulate the space, and thereby get the most out of it. Rethinking the shape of rooms doesn't have to mean making structural changes. If a room seems too long, for example, it could be possible to divide it in two with a screen or freestanding storage unit; if the ceiling seems too low, it is easily disguised by drawing attention away from it, using paint or furnishings, and onto the lower half of the room.

If it is necessary to move a wall, window, or doorway to improve the shape or size of a room, do not be put off. Generally this is not as difficult or expensive as it might sound (although you do have to own your home). The differences can be dramatic: a wall, knocked through to create

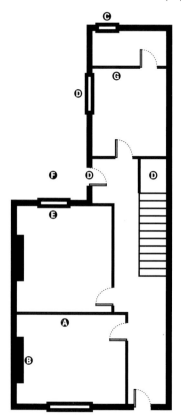

above **To visualize the effect of structural changes on a space, draw a scale plan of the rooms as they exist and use tracing overlays to try out alterations.**

an internal arch **A**, can open up a floor from front to back – increasing the versatility of the space and, potentially, the light flowing into it; blocking up a fireplace **B** or moving or enlarging a window **C** so that it frames a better view can completely alter the feel of a space; and relocating internal doors **D** can allow easier access to spaces or create new ones – such as an understairs room.

Other changes worth considering include turning windows that face onto a garden or patio into French doors **E**. If there is a side passage or yard, would a conservatory **F** make better use of the space? Would a small kitchen benefit from the knocking down of an internal wall **G** to enlarge it? And would it then be useful to install a breakfast bar?

It is always good to visualize the likely effects of changes before you carry them out. The easiest way to do this is to draw scale plans. Draw a plan for the whole floor, so that you can see how your changes will affect your home as a whole. You might like to use the design grids on pages 150–151. A scale of 1:48, where 1 inch represents 48 inches (4 feet), is usually suitable for this, but you can also use a 1:96 scale if your rooms are particularly large. Once you have drawn the existing layout, try out various structural changes by drawing alterations on a separate sheet of tracing paper overlay.

For a more three-dimensional preview, invest in a basic interior design computer software program. Even the cheapest allows you to view structural and also furniture layout changes from all sides, and "walk through" the rooms.

   A low-tech alternative used by many designers is to take photographs of the empty room and stick them together to offer a panoramic view. Once photocopied, this can be sketched over with marker pen.

RELATED PAGES

36 measuring
38 space planning
150 design grids

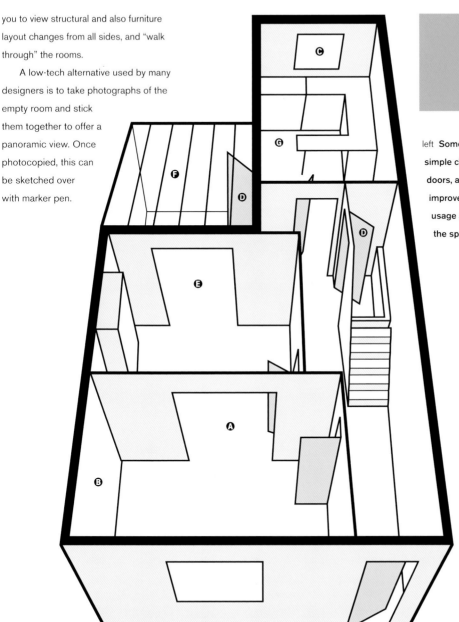

left **Some inexpensive, simple changes to walls, doors, and windows can improve considerably the usage and potential of the space in a home.**

deciding on your style

When decorating, deciding on a look can be the hardest part. If the fact that there are so many choices doesn't stop you in your tracks, then the fear that your decor will expose you as a raging snob or hopelessly uncool probably will. If nothing else, you will probably wonder how on earth a coherent look can be fashioned from the motley assortment of hand-me-downs and junk that passes for your furniture.

Establishing your style is a lot like learning a new language. The first time, you feel frustrated and worry about looking ridiculous when you try to say a few words. Once you've taken the plunge, however, you soon pick up the basics, which in turn does wonders for your confidence.

The process begins with a certain amount of learning by example. Look closely at rooms that appeal in some way, and identify those aspects or details that you like most. It could be the contrast of one color against another, or something seemingly minor, like a great door handle. Try also to describe the atmosphere. Do you feel relaxed or jumpy in there? Is there a sense of space, or are you hemmed in by clutter? Make a note of these thoughts because they will help you to focus on how you would like your home to look and feel.

It isn't just rooms that provide inspiration: the natural world, television programs, window displays, and fashion can be just as evocative, and for collectable visual reference the most accessible sources of all are, of course, books, magazines, and old photographs. (The plastic pocket in this book is a good place to store ideas as you collect them.)

compiling a mood board

When you are happy with your selection of pictures from magazines, photographs, etc., spread them out on a flat surface, paste them onto a sheet of cardboard, or stick them onto a large foldout sheet of paper. This is your mood board, and it will help you to see whether there is a pattern to your thoughts – it might be that certain colors recur or form a harmonious group, or that you discover a penchant for wicker furniture.

At some point further down the line, your mood board will probably turn out to be a useful source of paint colors, and a reassuring reminder that you're heading in the right direction. Right now, however, it is a great place to assess your ideas. You may well find that you're keen on very soft traditional sofas even though you're a self-proclaimed minimalist. Or that the rusty garden table found in your parents' garage would look great when paired with that magazine picture of canvas-covered chairs.

You will probably reject some of these ideas later, and modify others to suit your budget or as a result of new ideas and information, and that's fine too. The important point to remember is that you're no longer at square one.

RELATED PAGES

94 interpreting your mood board

97 home fact file: product choices

left Great decorating inspiration – in the form of color, shape, pattern, texture, and materials – appears everywhere. Whether you use a few initial sources or amass a pile of references, it won't be long before your style emerges.

planning the work

Start by making, or adding to, a list of structural, preparatory and decorative jobs to be done (see home fact file: structural changes on page 22) and make a budget breakdown, as shown here, to start estimating the costs involved. Fill in both the tasks and your costs in your home fact file, pages 42–51. Also using these pages, draw a scale floor plan for each room (see page 37). You may want to annotate these floor plans with the changes you have in mind.

Once you know what you would like to change about your home, the practicalities and the budget, it is time to establish a list of priorities. If you are planning to redecorate your home completely, and live there while you do so, it is best to tackle the room where everyone spends the most time first, so that there will be one oasis of calm amidst the chaos. This usually puts the kitchen at the top of the list, followed by the bathroom, bedrooms, living room and hall.

RELATED PAGES

22 structural changes

32 bringing in experts

41 home fact file: planning

planning a fast freshen-up

schedule

planning
Finalize changes ▸ Check that your landlord agrees with your proposed changes (if appropriate) ▸ Calculate the quantities of the materials needed and buy/order them

preparation
Remove furniture, carpets, curtains, etc. ▸ Cover fixed items with drop cloths ▸ Strip off or sand down old wallpaper or paintwork in the room ▸ Prepare old furniture for new paint or other decorative treatment ▸ Remove or loosen switch and outlet plates, door handles, window catches and curtain rods

decoration
Apply finishes to walls, ceilings, etc. ▸ Redecorate old furniture ▸ Replace curtain rods, outlets, etc. ▸ Rehang curtains, blinds and light fixtures ▸ Place furniture in position ▸ Hang pictures and mirrors

budget breakdown

planning

preparation
Cleaning materials	$ _____
Rental of wallpaper stripper, floor sander, etc.	$ _____
Tools and equipment (can these be begged or borrowed?)	$ _____

decoration
Decorating materials	$ _____
New hardware such as outlet plates, handles and curtain rods (can existing items be renovated?)	$ _____
Materials for updating furniture, curtains and other furnishings	$ _____
Lighting and accessories	$ _____

be realistic

You will soon realize that planning requires you to be detailed and flexible. It will be impossible to stick to an immovable schedule: some of your ideas may be impractical or unaffordable.

Don't overestimate your abilities either. If a job becomes more complex than you first thought, call in expert help – it could save you money in the long run. Remember that decorating always takes longer than you think. Be honest about the time you're able to devote.

Lastly, establish your budget and stick to it. Ensure that you have the money to complete a job before you start. And if holidays and eating out are important to you, then make sure that you can still afford them too.

planning a major overhaul

schedule

planning

Finalize design elements and discuss ideas with other household members ▶ Check structural changes with local government offices and obtain any permits ▶ Calculate the quantities of the materials needed and buy/order them ▶ Order custom-made items such as curtains and upholstered furniture, if buying new ▶ Clear the area ▶ Remove furniture, carpets, etc. and cover fixed items with dust sheets

structural changes

Demolish unwanted structural components, and strip out redundant plumbing, electric lines, etc. ▶ Remove building debris ▶ Install framing for new walls, floor or ceiling ▶ Install new utilities (outlets, plumbing, etc.) and insulation, if required ▶ Plaster new walls or ceilings; lay fixed floors such as tiles or wood strips; fix moldings such as baseboards and chair rails ▶ Hang doors and reglaze windows, if necessary ▶ Strip off old wallpaper or paintwork ▶ Install built-in furniture ▶ Connect radiators, appliances, bathtubs, sinks, etc.

decoration

Line walls, and prime and undercoat surfaces to be painted ▶ Apply final finishes (it's best to start with the ceiling and work downward) ▶ Fix switch and outlet plates, door handles and window catches ▶ Fix curtain rods ▶ Lay carpet and other sheet flooring ▶ Hang curtains or blinds ▶ Fix light fixtures ▶ Place furniture in position ▶ Hang pictures and mirrors

budget breakdown

planning

Obtaining permits	$ _____
Custom-made items	$ _____
	_____

structural changes

Contractors to demolish redundant structures/utilities and install replacements	$ _____
Trash disposal	$ _____
New building materials	$ _____
Contingency for unforeseen problems (allow 10–20% of total allocated to structural changes	$ _____
Materials for fixed floors, moldings, glazing, etc.	$ _____
Rental of professional tools	$ _____
Other tools and cleaning materials	$ _____

decoration

Built-in furniture	$ _____
Radiators, bathtubs, etc.	$ _____
Specialist contractors (for plumbing and electrics)	$ _____
Decorating materials	$ _____
Hardware (switches, door handles, curtain rods, etc.)	$ _____
New furniture	$ _____
Carpets, curtains, etc.	$ _____
Lighting and accessories	$ _____

bringing in experts

contacts

American Institute of Architects

1735 New York Avenue NW
Washington, DC 20006
202-626-7359
www.aia.org

American Society of Interior Designers

730 Fifth Avenue
New York, NY 10019
800-775-2743
www.interiors.org

International Association of Lighting Designers

200 World Trade Center,
Suite 487
Chicago, IL 60654
312-527-3677
www.iald.org

National Association of the Remodeling Industry

4900 Seminary Road,
Suite 320
Alexandria, VA 22311
800-440-6274
www.nari.org

National Association of Home Builders

1201 15th Street NW
Washington, DC 20005
800-368-5242
www.nahb.com

Some jobs really are best left to the experts. Major alterations to the fabric of your home, such as repairs to the roof or moving load-bearing walls, require both specialist skills and a great deal of experience, so don't take on a job of this size unless you know exactly what to expect and what it is going to cost you. Remember that even professional builders seldom do every job themselves – highly skilled jobs are left to roofing contractors, glaziers, and other specialists.

If you cannot afford to employ professionals to undertake major work, it is best to modify your plans and concentrate on making decorative improvements only. Thankfully, this has become easier than ever – home improvement stores are full of products that take the drudgery out of many DIY tasks, and bring specialist finishes and effects within the reach of every amateur. Even simple electrical and plumbing jobs can be attempted safely and with confidence.

who does what?

architects

If you are taking on a fixer-upper, a poorly laid out home, or a place that is too small (or too large) for your needs, architects can help you to make sense of the space. They will also prepare plans and working drawings, obtain the necessary permits, and help to find ways around legal problems that you may encounter. Once you have decided to go ahead, architects can also find and manage builders and contractors, and take on some (although not all) of the responsibility for ensuring that the job is completed within the agreed budget and time.

The best way to find the right architect is through recommendations. Always ask to see examples or photographs of work by two or three "possibles" before making your final choice, and bear in mind that you are about to forge an intimate working relationship with this person. Will you get along?

interior designers and decorators

Like architects, good designers are there to save you time and stress. They can make an independent, yet experienced, assessment of your home and lifestyle, and come up with decorative solutions that will look and function better, and even save money in the long run. They will have access to a much wider range of papers, fabrics, and other materials, and be able to find and supervise good contractors and craftspeople on your behalf. The best designers also understand that clients have great ideas of their own and often say that their role is simply to edit these and make them happen.

Magazines and the design pages of weekend newspapers are good places to start the search for a designer. Alternatively, contact professional organizations (see the contacts boxes on these pages).

building contractors

A good building contractor will happily do jobs as diverse as removing and putting up walls, laying flooring, installing new heating ducts, and boxing in pipes. No contractor, however, will undertake any and every task (and you should be suspicious of those who claim to be able to).

Here, too, personal recommendation counts for a great deal. If this isn't possible, ask prospective contractors for details of two or more previous clients, and contact them to find out if they were happy with the work and service provided.

electricians

If an electrical job consists of more than a cosmetic change (such as replacing switch plates) or routine maintenance, it is best to leave it to a professional electrician. For obvious safety reasons, make sure he or she belongs to a recognized professional association and that the work complies with building codes.

plumbers

Many common plumbing tasks, such as replacing a faucet or clearing drains, are simple enough to be carried out by anyone. However, sanitary plumbing and drainage should comply with building codes and is therefore best left to a professional, as is the installation of equipment such as hot water tanks and showers, in order to prevent water waste and possible contamination.

painters and decorators

There are very few painting and decorating tasks that you should not undertake yourself, as long as you have the right equipment and can master one or two very simple techniques. Ceilings are inevitably harder to paint than walls. To create a safe platform to work from, you will need to rent a couple of sturdy scaffold boards and rest them between two stepladders or trestles.

However, you may prefer to leave painting to professionals if you suffer from any breathing problems or allergies to solvents and other chemicals.

furniture and cabinet makers

Having built-in, custom-made storage isn't something that only the rich can afford to do: you could well find that it costs little or no more than buying similar nonfitted items off the shelf, especially when cheaper materials such as plywood and medium density fiberboard (MDF) are used. In a small or awkwardly shaped space, it is also the most efficient option.

Contractors and architects can often recommend good furniture and cabinet makers, and magazines are a good alternative source to commission young designers. Nowadays, it is also much easier than before to find upholstered furniture manufacturers who will alter their standard sizes of sofas and chairs to fit your space, at little or no extra cost.

National Kitchen and Bath Association
687 Willow Grove St.
Hackettstown, NJ 07840
800-410-6522
www.nkba.com

National Association of Plumbing-Heating-Cooling Contractors
P.O. Box 6808
180 S. Washington Street
Falls Church, VA 22040
800-533-7694 or
703-237-8100
www.naphcc.org

National Electrical Contractors Association
3 Bethesda Metro Center,
Suite 1100
Bethesda, MD 20814
301-657-3110
www.necanet.org

Floor Installation Association of North America (FIANA)
P.O. Box 5505
Granbury, TX 76049
888-883-4262
www.fiana.org

- ▶ Are there conditions attached that would allow the contractor to disclaim responsibility for damage or losses?
- ▶ Check that each contractor intends to complete the work to the same standard.
- ▶ Are there any useful inclusions? Is the cost of organizing trash disposal a part of one of the quotes, for example?

getting the work done

be specific

A written specification of what you want done and relevant drawings are vital. If you should change your mind later, be sure to do so in writing, and ask contractors to notify you of any additional costs in writing too. Don't expect contractors to make design decisions for you (it is bound to lead to misunderstandings), and be as clear and detailed as possible about how you expect the end result to look.

above **Major structural changes, such as the making of a recess or the installation of plumbing and wiring, can transform the way you use a room. Such changes can be complex and are best left to the experts.**

agreeing on terms

estimates

Where possible and appropriate, ask two or three builders or contractors to provide estimates for the job. They will need copies of your list of jobs to be done and room plans, and you will need to agree on a start date, the length of the contract, and the price.

awarding the job

The estimates are bound to vary, so examine them in detail. The more detailed you can be about your needs, the easier it will be to make direct comparisons.

   Your final choice may be the person or firm who turns out to be the cheapest; it may be the one who can do the job fastest; or it may simply be the one you get along with best.

- ▶ Do any give you a written time schedule?
- ▶ Are the same quantities of materials included in each quote?

payments

A good contractor will not mind being paid at the end of the job, as long as it is fairly small. However, you will probably need to make interim payments on jobs that last for more than, say, four weeks. Agree on what these will be before work begins. In addition, tell your contractor at the outset that you plan to retain up to 10 percent of the total cost for three to six months after completion, to cover the cost of any defects caused by faulty work.

working safely

reminders

- Only qualified professionals should carry out major work involving gas and electricity.
- Plan ahead – make sure you have all the correct tools and materials on hand before you start a job.
- Protect yourself – wear protective clothing and gloves, and safety equipment such as goggles and face masks if using chemicals or where dust is likely to be created.
- Always follow the manufacturer's instructions supplied with tools; keep them clean and in good repair.
- Tidy up as you work: piles of trash can be tripped over.
- When painting or cleaning, keep oil- or solvent-stained rags spread out and aired (crumpled-up rags can spontaneously ignite if they get too warm). Store dirty rags in water until they can be disposed of.
- Never mix cleaning solutions or chemicals.
- Never smoke while working.
- All equipment and materials should be stored out of the reach of children.
- Place a ladder on an even, solid surface, and at the correct angle; make sure it is the right size for the job; never use one with loose or missing rungs.
- Cutting tools should only be used on a table or bench that has been designed for the job.
- Always wear leather or similarly thick gloves when using power tools.
- Use a pipe and cable detector before drilling into walls or floors.

- Always turn off electrical circuits at the fuse box before working with light fixtures, switches, or outlets.
- Don't attempt potentially dangerous jobs when alone. If an accident occurs, a second person can get help right away.
- Familiarize yourself with basic first aid techniques and keep a properly stocked kit in an easy to find place.

below **Access to wine storage and high cupboards has been designed with safety in mind. This hooked ladder and fitted rail are secure and also stylish.**

measuring

Even if you only intend to give a room a coat of paint and rearrange the furniture, a scale plan will come in useful. If at all possible, take measurements and draw the plans up before you move in. It is much easier to measure a room when it is empty, and you will be able to check that the doors, windows, and staircases are large enough to move large and bulky items through. (If the building has an elevator, it's a good idea to measure this too, for the same reason.)

taking measurements

Accurate measurements are vital, so take them with care. Remember to note the direction in which the doors and windows swing open, the positions of heating registers or radiators, switches, and outlets, and the dimensions of moldings such as cornices and baseboards.

You will need a pencil and eraser, notepad, retractable tape measure, stepladder and camera (optional).

❶ sketch the room

Place yourself in the center of the room and draw a rough sketch of its shape. Include any fixed features, such as fireplaces and window bays. Also mark in outlets and heating registers or radiators. If you have a camera, photograph as much of the room as you can.

❷ take the wall and floor dimensions

Measure and record on your plan the length of each wall in turn, at a point about 3 ft above floor level. Incidentally, this helps to check whether the walls are parallel.

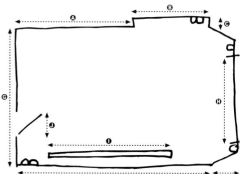

Next, measure the length and width of the room at floor level, and add these to your sketch plan. Then measure the room diagonally from corner to corner to check that it is square (rooms seldom are). Remember to record the depths of recesses and openings.

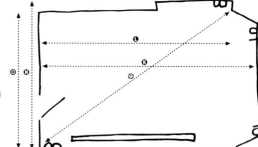

right above **Measure the lengths of walls (A, B, D, F, G), including recess depths (C, E), and key features such as door (J), window (H), and radiator (I) widths.**

right below **Take the floor dimensions: measure the length and width of the floor (L, O) including recesses (K, N). Also measure the diagonal (M).**

❸ draw the elevations

Face each wall in turn, and draw a sketch of each on separate sheets of paper. Stand on a stepladder to measure the wall height from floor to ceiling. Next, measure and note the dimensions of doors, windows, alcoves, and moldings. Carefully mark the positions of radiators, switches, etc. on each elevation. (The measurements indicated on the drawing below are particularly useful for making curtains and blinds. See "calculating quantities" on page 40.)

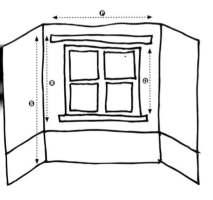

drawing plans to scale

Use the gridded pages provided on pages 42–51 to draw accurate scale plans of each room. Each ¹⁄₁₆-inch square can be made to represent 1 inch in real life (i.e., scale 1:16); 3 inches (scale 1:48) or 6 inches (1:96). Use the largest scale possible, for the greatest accuracy.

You will need a sharp pencil, ink pen with a fine nib or point, square, and ruler or scale rule.

❶ transfer the floor plan

Using light pencil marks, transfer the measurements on your sketch floor plan to the grid. Once you are happy with the outline, draw over it in ink, then indicate the doors, windows, fixed features, and outlets. Note the measurements around the outside of your plan for easy reference.

❷ repeat for the elevations

Transfer your sketch elevations to the grid if you have space (or photocopy the grids before you start). These elevations can be used to determine the postitioning of curtain rods, new moldings etc.

left A simple elevation drawing, with dimensions recorded (P, Q, R, S), is invaluable for calculating quantities of surface materials and window dressing fabrics.

below Draw up a scale version of your plan along with key measurements. You may choose to annotate this further with your ideas for structural and decorative changes.

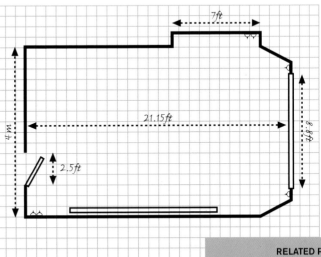

RELATED PAGES

40 calculating quantities
41 home fact file: planning

space planning

One of the most useful things about having scale plans of individual rooms is that they allow you to work out where furniture, storage, and other features will go. To experiment with furniture layouts, draw a plan of each room at a scale of 1:24, where 1 inch represents 24 inches (2 ft). Next, cut out cardboard shapes to the same scale to represent your furniture and fixtures. (If you use the plans you have drawn on pages 42–51, your furniture shapes must be drawn to the same scale as your rooms.) You will need tracing paper, masking tape, a soft pencil and eraser, and a ruler or square. Alternatively, use overlays of tracing paper. These methods will allow you to move furniture around to your heart's content and are surprisingly good at warning you of potential problems: you will be able to tell, for example, if placing a shelving unit near the window is likely to partially block the light, or make it difficult to close the curtains. Try out different arrangements until you find the one that works best for you.

A Backlighting of computer screen gives poor visibility.

B Cabinet wastes space.

C Lamp cord trails dangerously across floor.

D Wardrobe blocks light.

E Dressing table positioned too near door.

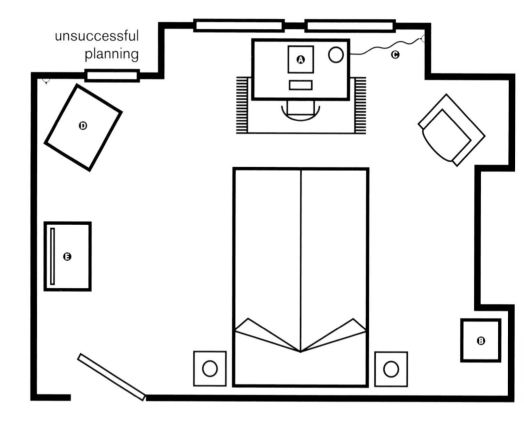

unsuccessful planning

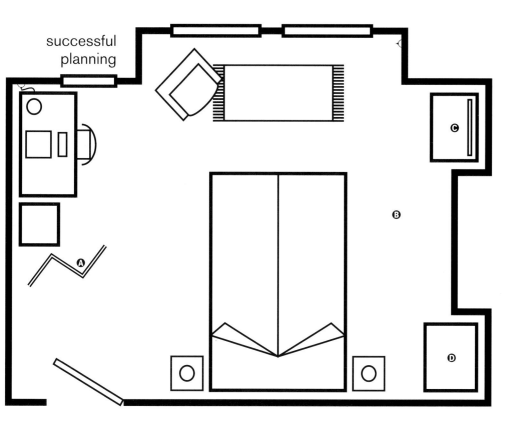

successful planning

priorities

When designing a room layout for the first time, you may need some guidance when positioning furniture. It can help to consider allocation of space to furniture and features in the following order:

❶ major items of furniture

Place large items, such as sofas and desks, close to windows if the room is to be used during the day. To increase the sense of privacy in a bedroom, try to place the bed so that it is partially concealed behind the opening door. Remember to allow space around each item for cleaning and outstretched legs.

❷ storage

If regular access is needed, there should be enough space to open closet doors and drawers. Also, think about what the storage is needed for. For example, do you need to store certain items next to a desk? Would the kitchen be easier to use if you could swap the contents of cupboards around to store pans and/or ingredients next to the stove?

❸ lighting

Plug-in lamps should be placed where there is no danger of tripping over cords, and so that the light can be directed to where it is needed.

Ⓐ Clearly defined work area with good lighting from window and lamp.
Ⓑ Good circulation space.
Ⓒ Dressing table makes good use of alcove and gets best of natural light.
Ⓓ Wardrobe fits snugly into alcove space.

RELATED PAGES

80 manipulating space
84 placing furniture
173 symbols for plans

calculating quantities

window treatments

The amount of fabric needed varies with the style. It is valuable to have the following measurements on hand:
- Length of the curtain rod or track.
- Distance from the curtain rod or track to the floor.
- Distance from the rod or track to the sill.
- Height and width of the window.
- Height and width of the window recess.
- Distance between the top of the window frame and the lower edge of the cornice or the ceiling (to ensure there is space for curtain rod brackets).

The room measurements noted on your plans (pages 42–51) enable you to work out how much paint and paper you are going to need. Take them with you when you go shopping to avoid buying too much or, worse, not enough.

paint for walls

Calculate the surface area of each wall by multiplying the length by the height, then add these together to get the total wall area for the room. As a rough guide, 1 gallon of paint will cover approximately 250–400 square feet. Remember that you may need more than one coat.

wallpaper

Add the lengths of each wall together to arrive at a total perimeter measurement. Measure the height from the baseboard to the dado, chair rail or cornice, and calculate quantities using the table below.

finishes for woodwork and moldings

The covering power of semigloss paint, wood stains and varnishes varies a great deal. Also an ornate molding will require more paint than a simple one. As a very rough guide, however, a 6-foot run of molding has a surface area of 1 square foot. One gallon of gloss paint will cover 300–400 square feet. Once again, you may need to allow for more than one coat.

floor finishes

The floor area can simply be calculated by multiplying the length by the width. If there are several sections, do this for each and add the amounts together. If you plan to lay ceramic or terra-cotta tiles, allow 10 percent extra for breakages with a plain design, and 15 to 20 percent extra with a patterned one.

ceiling finishes

Unless you have a sloping or vaulted ceiling, its area should be the same as for the floor. To calculate the area of a sloping ceiling, multiply the length by the width. To estimate wallpaper rolls required for a ceiling, divide the area in square feet by 36.

	total perimeter measurement of walls in the room												
no. of 18 in x 24 ft rolls needed	32 ft	36 ft	40 ft	44 ft	48 ft	52 ft	56 ft	60 ft	64 ft	68 ft	72 ft	76 ft	80 ft
8 ft	8	9	10	11	12	13	14	15	16	17	18	19	20
9 ft	9	10	11	12	14	15	16	17	18	19	20	21	22
10 ft	10	11	12	14	15	16	17	19	20	21	22	23	25

height of room to be papered

home fact file
planning

Use the following pages to record the dimensions of your rooms. Draw plans for each area of your home, following the method explained on pages 36–37, and annotate them as suggested. Summarize your initial decorating ideas by listing the materials and items that you have in mind, such as "paint the walls a soft blue-gray"; "lay natural flooring"; "fix blinds." Noting your initial cost estimates, too, will help you to prepare a budget.

living room

work plan

measurements

maximum room length and width:

ceiling height:

window size(s):

door size(s):

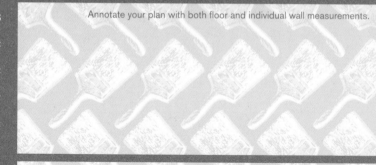

Annotate your plan with both floor and individual wall measurements.

decorating materials

walls and ceilings:

floor:

doors:

windows:

furniture and furnishings:

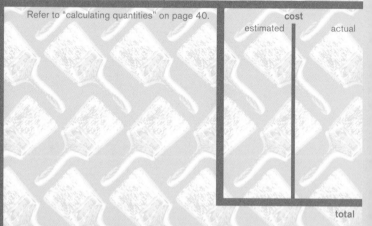

Use this space to outline your ideas for colors and materials. To detail final product choices, use pages 98–111.

quantities and cost

walls and ceiling:

floor:

doors:

windows:

furniture and furnishings:

Refer to "calculating quantities" on page 40.

cost

estimated   actual

total

kitchen/dining room

measurements

maximum room length and width:

ceiling height:

window size(s):

door size(s):

Annotate your plan with both floor and individual wall measurements.

decorating materials

walls and ceilings:

floor:

doors:

windows:

furniture and furnishings:

Use this space to outline your ideas for colors and materials.
To detail final product choices, use pages 98–111.

quantities and cost

walls and ceiling:

floor:

doors:

windows:

furniture and furnishings:

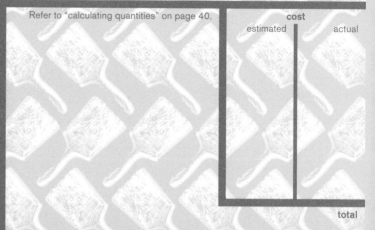

Refer to "calculating quantities" on page 40.

cost

estimated   actual

total

bedroom

work plan

measurements

maximum room length and width:

ceiling height:

window size(s):

door size(s):

Annotate your plan with both floor and individual wall measurements.

decorating materials

walls and ceilings:

floor:

doors:

windows:

furniture and furnishings:

Use this space to outline your ideas for colors and materials.
To detail final product choices, use pages 98–111.

quantities and cost

walls and ceiling:

floor:

doors:

windows:

furniture and furnishings:

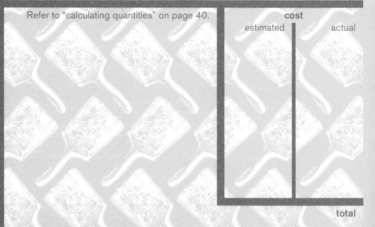

Refer to "calculating quantities" on page 40.

cost

estimated   actual

total

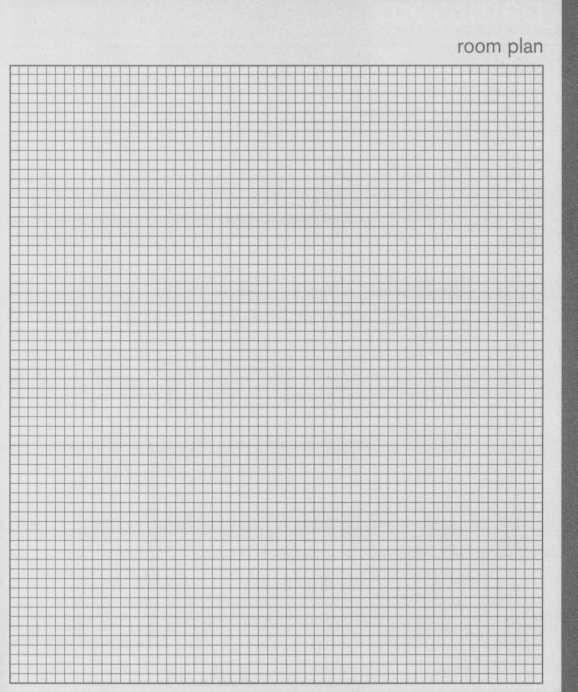

bathroom

work plan

measurements

maximum room length and width:

ceiling height:

window size(s):

door size(s):

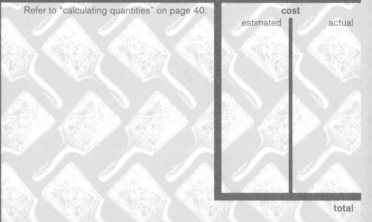

Annotate your plan with both floor and individual wall measurements.

decorating materials

walls and ceilings:

floor:

doors:

windows:

furniture and furnishings:

Use this space to outline your ideas for colors and materials. To detail final product choices, use pages 98–111.

quantities and cost

walls and ceiling:

floor:

doors:

windows:

furniture and furnishings:

Refer to "calculating quantities" on page 40.

cost	
estimated	actual

total

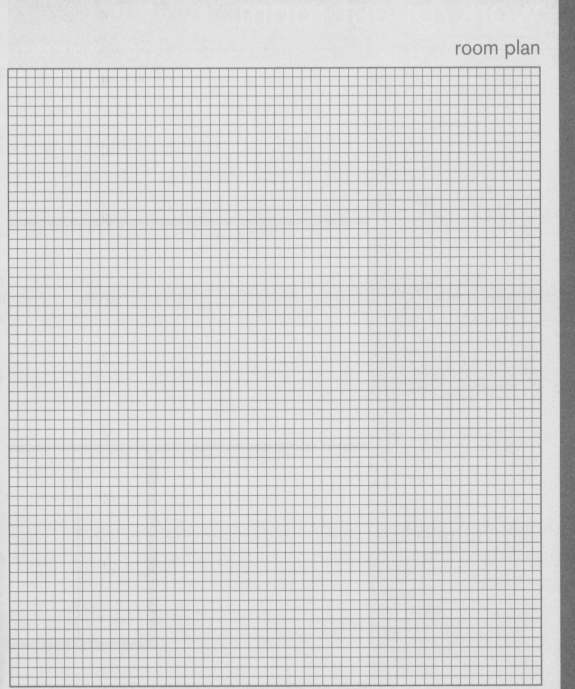

work /guest room

measurements

Annotate your plan with both floor and individual wall measurements.

maximum room length and width:

ceiling height:

window size(s):

door size(s):

decorating materials

Use this space to outline your ideas for colors and materials. To detail final product choices, use pages 98–111.

walls and ceilings:

floor:

doors:

windows:

furniture and furnishings:

quantities and cost

Refer to "calculating quantities" on page 40.

walls and ceiling:

floor:

doors:

windows:

furniture and furnishings:

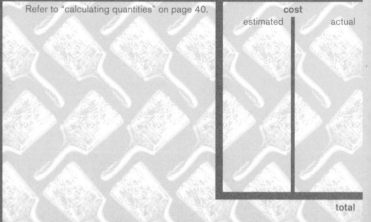

	cost	
	estimated	actual

total

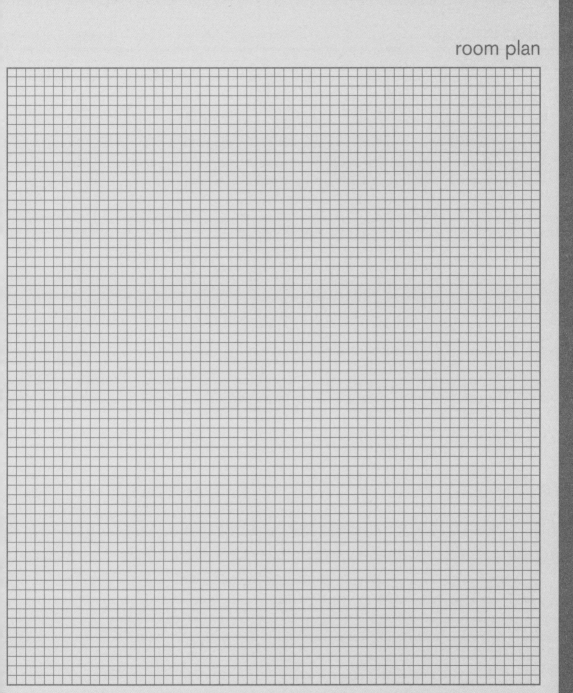

preparation

renovate and repair

above **Evidence of wear and tear can add character to a building and is worth retaining as long as it doesn't make your home unsafe or impractical.**

For many renovation and repair tasks all you need is a basic set of tools and one of the many home maintenance manuals available. It goes without saying that repairs and maintenance should be carried out before starting to decorate.

structural faults

Large cracks in walls, damp patches, musty smells, and bulging plasterwork are some of the signs that all is not well with the structure of your home. If these have not already been assessed in an official house inspection, you should call in an expert to assess the scale of such problems, and take action as soon as possible. Features that appear to be in poor condition – for example, a door on which the hinges have worked loose – aren't necessarily beyond saving. Hinges can be retightened, and woodwork and moldings can be repaired or replaced. Likewise, many surfaces, such as plasterwork or tiling, can be repaired in patches.

dampness

Water is one of a building's worst enemies. The repair of any areas where it collects should be a priority. Check bathtub and sink edges and kitchen countertops, to ensure that they are properly sealed. If possible, also look underneath sinks and bathtubs, and behind appliances such as washing machines, to see whether there are leaks in the pipes. Water also collects by condensing on cold windows, and it can damage the frames. Most home improvement stores sell a variety of easy-to-use products that will help to avoid or treat such problems.

insulation

General repair tasks might include weatherproofing and making sure that windows and doors open and shut properly. Adequate insulation for your plumbing and heating systems is another must, both to save energy and prevent winter freeze-ups.

fixtures and furniture

The sense of pride that comes from fixing a sticking drawer, silencing a squeak, or steadying a wobble, is out of all proportion to the time or skill it takes.

If you visit junk shops or follow up sales through newspaper advertisements, or are ever offered other people's cast-offs, get into the habit of carrying a tape measure around with you, so that you can check and record the vital statistics of any item before you accept it. Remember to check for problems such as woodworm and missing parts. It also pays to compare prices across various sources. You could well find that items are cheaper in stores that specialize in a particular field, whether it's ex-office furniture or old sofas, because the owners of these places have large stocks of similar items. Don't expect to find many bargains if you're after pieces that are trendy or collectable.

above Old bathroom fixtures have an appealing sturdiness and a generosity of scale. They can still be bought cheaply, but be prepared to spend a fair amount of time and money on renovation.

RELATED PAGES

60 preparing woodwork

66 seasonal changes

172 home maintenance checklist

tool kit

It is impossible to have your own place and not need a basic tool kit. Sooner or later, you will need a screwdriver to make a minor repair, or a hammer to put up pictures, and it's worth making sure you have the right one. Buy the best tools that you can afford, and look after them: this means keeping them clean and sharp and, most importantly, knowing where they are.

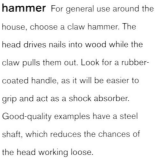

glue gun

cordless drill A cordless drill that can also be used as a power screwdriver will make light work of putting up shelves and a thousand other jobs around the house. It's also ideal for use in areas without a power supply, such as the attic or garden. Make sure you can hold it comfortably in one hand, and that it has variable speeds for drilling different materials, a reverse function (handy for removing screws), and a hammer action for drilling into brick and concrete.

drill bits Three basic types of drill bits are available, each for use with different materials: wood, masonry, and metal.

glue gun You'll find all sorts of uses for a glue gun, especially for light repairs and small projects such as customizing furniture and accessories.

hammer For general use around the house, choose a claw hammer. The head drives nails into wood while the claw pulls them out. Look for a rubber-coated handle, as it will be easier to grip and act as a shock absorber. Good-quality examples have a steel shaft, which reduces the chances of the head working loose.

claw hammer

hot air gun Also known as a heat gun, this is worth investing in if you plan to strip large areas of painted or varnished woodwork. It works by melting the layers of paint to be stripped and is preferable to chemical strippers if you are allergic to the solvents contained in them. Hot air guns can also be used to speed up paint or varnish drying over small areas, to bend plastic pipes, and to solder plumbing joints.

pliers Use pliers for cutting electrical wire, and gripping small or awkwardly placed nails and screws.

disc sander Electric sanders can remove old decorated wood surfaces quickly, while offering the control of precision sanding. Modern disc sanders come with a variety of fittings, allowing access to corners and odd shapes, such as moldings.

saws: hand saws Two types of saw should pretty well cover your needs. A tenon saw, for cleanly cutting small sections of lumber (such as battens) to size, and for slicing through thin sheet materials such as plywood. A hacksaw, with its tiny teeth and open frame, is ideally suited to cutting through metal and pipes.

hot air gun

materials), and some can be connected to a vacuum cleaner for improved dust collection.

screwdrivers You will use these more often than any other tool, so choose those with large, easy-to-grip handles. A kit containing slot and Philips-head screwdrivers in a variety of sizes is ideal – buy one that contains stubby versions, for use in confined spaces, if possible.

saws: jigsaw Invest in a jigsaw to cut wood, thin metal, and plastic effortlessly along both straight and curved lines. More expensive models allow you to cut at an angle to create bevelled or mitered edges, to regulate the speed (useful when cutting very thin

spirit level This is essential to ensure that shelves are horizontal and uprights are vertical. Lightweight metal models are easiest to handle, and the most versatile examples have a v-shaped groove for balancing on pipes and poles.

Use a retractable model for safety, and change the blade frequently. When accuracy is of prime importance, use it instead of a pencil for marking sheet materials such as wood and hardboard.

jigsaw

orbital sander

tape measure
A retractable steel tape measure is essential when you're decorating. Use it to measure rooms, to check the dimensions of furniture when out shopping, and to make sure that you cut materials and wallpaper to the right size. Choose a 25-ft model with a hooked tip and button to lock the measure in place.

trimming knife For cutting wallpaper, stencils, carpet, and other floorings, a trimming knife is invaluable.

tool tips

▸ Store tools in a box or bag designed for the purpose.
▸ Specialized power tools save time and effort, and they can be rented cheaply for short periods.
▸ If using tools for long periods, wear sturdy gloves to protect your hands.
▸ Don't force tools to do jobs that they weren't designed for: it's the easiest way to put them out of action and can be dangerous.

preparing walls

Thorough preparation of walls always improves the final look, but a smooth base takes time and effort to achieve. The process can be sped up if you are happy to settle for a less-than-perfect finish. However, you will still need to wash down walls and fill any cracks or holes.

tools • stripping knife or paint scraper • steam wallpaper stripper • hard toothbrush • caulking gun • filling knife

materials • interior-grade filler • general purpose sandpaper • stabilizing primer • flexible acrylic sealant

1 With a stripping knife or scraper, score the surface of the old wallpaper into sections. This makes it easier to remove the paper once you have steamed it. Try to avoid scoring too deeply, as this will damage the surface of the wall below.

2 Soften the wallpaper with a steam wallpaper stripper. Work over approximately one square yard at a time, and remove the sections of loosening paper with a stripping knife. Brush out all visible cracks,

previously painted walls

There is no need for additional preparation if you're planning to apply a new layer of paint over previously painted walls, although you may need to apply three coats if you're painting a light shade over a dark color. The same applies to reapplications of whitewashed and distemper finishes, but they will need to be scrubbed off and stabilized with a sealer if you want to switch to an painted finish. Semigloss paint should always be rubbed down with sandpaper before repainting.

chips, and holes to remove any loose dirt and plaster. Once all the paper has been removed, make up a solution of warm water and a little household detergent and wash down the walls to remove any remaining dirt and fragments of paper.

3 Fill any cleaned-out cracks and holes generously with an all-purpose interior-grade filler. Smooth down the surface with a filling knife, but leave the filler slightly raised above the surface so that it can be rubbed down once it has dried. Leave to dry.

4 Rub down the filled areas with general purpose sandpaper to obtain a smooth, even finish. If the walls are very dusty after being rubbed down, it may be necessary to treat them with a stabilizing primer. If your walls have been newly plastered, you will need to seal the surface with an acrylic primer before applying any paint. Lastly, seal any gaps between the walls and baseboards with a caulking gun and flexible acrylic sealant.

preparing woodwork

Interior woodwork is subjected to a fair amount of wear and tear – just think how many times you touch a door – so thorough preparation of surfaces is essential. Needless to say, smooth surfaces collect less dirt, are easier to clean, and they look better, too.

tools • polyethylene sheeting • rubber gloves • narrow decorator's brush • paint scraper • scrub pad • palette or table knife • clean rags • medium-grade sandpaper

materials • chemical paint stripper • soapy water • interior-grade wood filler • knot sealer

1 Before you begin, remove all handles, hooks, brassware, catches, etc., and lay down newspaper or polyethylene sheeting to protect your work area. Work in a well-ventilated room, and always wear rubber gloves when handling caustic solutions such as paint stripper. Apply the paint stripper following the manufacturer's instructions. Use a narrow decorator's brush to work the stripper into corners and fine moldings.

2 Once the paint begins to soften and bubble, remove it using a paint scraper.

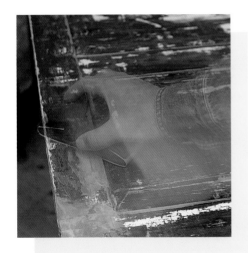

using a blowtorch or heat gun

Old paint can also be removed with a blowtorch or heat gun, together with a combination shave hook. Start at the bottom of the area to be stripped, so that the heat can help to soften the paint above as it rises. Place a heatproof container or suitable material under the area to be stripped to catch any hot fragments. Keep the heat source moving continually to reduce the risk of scorching. Fill and smooth as before.

Keep your gloves on while doing this. Always strip along the grain of the wood and, where possible, strip moldings first, then panels and flat areas. Once you have stripped the wood, wash down the surface with soapy water using a nylon scrub pad. This should remove any remaining paint. Then leave the wood to dry.

3 Using a palette knife or table knife, fill any damaged areas or cracks with interior-grade wood filler. This is available in several colors, so choose one that more or less matches the color of the surrounding wood if you plan to varnish or leave it bare.

Level the filler with a clean, damp rag while it is still malleable. Paint any knots with knot sealer to stop resin from seeping through your new paint finish.

4 Finally, sand any rough patches using medium-grade sandpaper. Once you have obtained a smooth finish, you can apply your varnish or paint as required.

sanding floorboards

As most wooden floors are made of strips or planks, it is virtually impossible to achieve a perfectly smooth finish prior to painting or varnishing. The good news is that this matters less than with walls or furniture. Instead, the key to successful preparation lies in sanding the surface.

tools • pliers • claw hammer • center punch • safety goggles • face mask • power and edging sanders (both with built-in dust collection if possible) • different grades of sandpaper (as advised, to fit sander) • vacuum cleaner • scrub brush

1 Clear the room of all movable objects. Nail down any loose floorboards and remove protruding nails with pliers or a claw hammer. If they cannot be pulled out, punch them below the surface of the wood with a hammer and a center punch. You must make sure that the surface of the floor is free from any obstructions before you begin sanding.

2 Before you start to sand, seal off the room because wood dust travels far! Wear safety goggles and a face mask at all times. First fit a coarse sandpaper. Always lift the front of the sander before switching it on – this stops it

chemical stripping

If you can't bear the thought of vacuuming all that dust, and only need to strip a small area, such as stair treads, consider using a chemical stripper. Several types are available, but one of the most effective can be made at home, simply by mixing caustic soda with water, and thickening the liquid with flour or cornstarch. Use with care: wear rubber gloves, safety goggles, and a rubber apron, and work in a well-ventilated room. Small patches of varnish can also be removed by scrubbing with mineral spirits.

from gouging out the wood – and lower it slowly as you begin to push it forward for sanding. Some power sanders have a lever to make this easier.

3 Start in one corner of the room, and sand the floor in diagonal strips that slightly overlap one another. Once you have covered the whole floor, sand along the diagonal in the other direction, in the same way. Next, fit a finer sandpaper, and sand along the direction of the wood grain to even out the finish. Vacuum up any escaped dust as you go along.

This should be sufficient to remove all the old finish, along with stains or accretions. Some filling may also be necessary to level off deep holes and repair any damaged areas. For instructions on how to repair holes in woodwork see "preparing woodwork" on page 60.

4 Use an edging sander to sand right up to the baseboards and into the corners. Again, try to use a model with dust collection. Finish by scrubbing the floor with water and a little bleach. Allow to dry thoroughly.

preparing metalwork

A wide range of metals, from aluminum to wrought iron, can be found in most homes, and it's difficult to imagine contemporary interiors without stainless steel. Some metals are meant to be left bare, but others need a coat of paint to keep them free of rust and discoloration.

tools • safety goggles • safety gloves • wire brush or an attachment for a power drill • paintbrushes

materials • emery paper • cloth • turpentine • rust inhibitor • epoxy-based filler • aluminum mesh (if required, for filling larger holes) • metal primer • gloss or enamel paint (formulated for exterior use as required)

1 When preparing rusted and/or flaking painted metalwork for fresh painting, always wear safety goggles and gloves for protection, as flakes of paint or rust have a tendency to fly around when being removed. Use a wire brush and emery paper to remove all the rust and old paint (a wire brush attachment to a power drill will help to speed up the process and is particularly useful for tackling tight corners; various sizes of brush and grades of emery paper are available).

alternative action

If your painted metalwork is in good condition, there is no need to remove old paint layers before repainting, unless the layers have already built up to such an extent that it is difficult to open and shut the windows. Simply clean the old paint with detergent and water, sand the surface with fine sandpaper, then apply a suitable primer and paint. If you are painting new copper pipes, clean them with turpentine before painting with oil paint.

Note: Do not attempt to use a hot air gun, as it will simply heat up the metal and bake the paint on, making removal extremely difficult.

2 Clean the sanded metalwork with a cloth using turpentine to remove all traces of dirt, dust, and grease. Paint rust inhibitor onto any bare or rusty patches – make sure it soaks thoroughly into any boltheads, hinges, and joints.

3 Fill any holes or pits with an epoxy-based filler. This not only helps to provide a level surface for painting, but also acts as a rust inhibitor. If there are large holes, you may need to back them with some aluminum mesh to provide an anchor for the filler. Take care to mix just a little filler at a time, as it hardens quickly.

4 Once the filler is dry, apply a metal primer to prevent further rusting. Apply gloss or enamel paint in thin layers. If the metalwork is to be left outside, ensure that the primer and paints are specially formulated for exterior use.

seasonal changes

Just like their inhabitants, buildings and furnishings are affected by the weather, by atmospheric pollution, and by the changing seasons. Helping your home respond to changes in seasons will ensure that it feels comfortable all the year round, just as dressing differently allows your body to cope with different temperatures.

in the spring

You know the weather is improving when the state of the windows grabs your attention. Brighter sunshine reveals grimy glass, curtains, or blinds, all of which can be cleaned without difficulty. When, with a rise in temperature, you decide that you want to open the windows, you may find them stuck – either because the woodwork has swelled up, or because they have been covered with layers of paint, or they may even have been permanently screwed shut for security.

To determine the cause, first work a stripping knife around the edge of the window – this will help to break any hardened paint layers. If this doesn't make any difference, run your fingers over the window to see if there are any screws embedded in the woodwork. If there are, scrape the paint away from the screwheads and remove. If the window still doesn't open, the wood is probably swollen. Hinged windows can be loosened by tapping around the edge opposite the hinges with a hammer and a small piece of wood. Once the window is free, strip all the old paint from the edges and allow the wood to dry. Use a block plane to shave some wood from the sticking edges. Fill any damaged areas, then prime and paint to seal.

summertime

At the height of summer, the sun will need to be kept out of your home to stop it from overheating. In addition, bright sunlight quickly damages paintings, fabrics, and furniture. Closing blinds, curtains, or shutters during the day will help, and good ventilation will also moderate rises in temperature.

below **Lightweight curtains can look wonderfully ethereal in a bedroom. If early morning light concerns you, team them with practical light-excluding blinds.**

get ready for winter

It's a good idea to check that your heating system works, and to get it serviced if necessary, before the cold weather really sets in. If you have working fireplaces, have them swept (do this before decorating if possible), and check the fireback and chimney for damage.

Central heating dries out the air, and this can cause the joints in wooden floors and furniture to move. It can be helpful to replace some of the moisture by using a humidifier, placing bowls of water or vases of flowers around, and by opening the windows.

Rooms shouldn't be allowed to get damp, as this encourages air-borne fungal spores to grow, causing telltale brown stains on walls. If nothing is done about dampness, it will eventually damage the building's structure.

To keep water out, the roof, walls, doorways, and window openings must be kept in good repair, and gutters kept free of blockages so that water cannot collect there.

Good ventilation is the most effective way to regulate moisture levels indoors. Condensation will also drop if rooms are kept warm. Weatherproofing doors and windows helps to keep heat inside, and it

may be worth using insulating decorating materials such as cork and paper-backed fabrics on cold walls. Also consider lining walls with insulating plasterboard, or even tongue-and-groove paneling with a layer of mineral wool insulation behind.

We rely more on artificial lighting during the winter too. It can never match the subtlety of daylight, but you can vary the effects created by using several light sources and shades and dimmers.

Other decorative ways to increase comfort levels in winter include using warm colors and rich textures or patterns.

above **To warm up an all-white room in the winter, make sure it's draft-free, and add temporary touches of red or brown in the form of furnishings or accessories.**

cleaning: the structure

Every decorating job begins with a good cleaning. Surface grease, dust, and dirt have to be removed before any new finishes are applied. A deep cleaning can also work miracles on old fixtures such as door handles and kitchen appliances. Getting rid of the grime reveals their character and could well be the only renovation they need.

bathroom fixtures Stains and scratches on acrylic bathtubs can be removed by rubbing gently with a metal cleaner. Buff well once the mark has gone.

To remove stains on enameled bathtubs, try rubbing with kerosene or turpentine, then rinse with dishwashing liquid in hot water. Avoid using conventional bathtub cleaning products, unless specifically approved, as they contain abrasives that will dull the bathtub's surface.

ceramic and terra-cotta tiled floors Ceramic and glazed terra-cotta tiled floors are easily cleaned using a floor mop dipped in a solution of household cleaner. Remove as much water as possible.

Unglazed terra-cotta tiles may need to be scrubbed with a stiff brush and a stronger solution of household cleaner.

fireplaces Rust spots can be removed from cast-iron fire surrounds with a wire brush, steel wool, or a chemical rust remover. Other materials, such as stone, slate, and marble, can be given a general cleaning with diluted household cleaner, but badly stained sections may need the services of a professional.

linoleum and vinyl floors Use a mop and a weak solution of an all-purpose cleaner on these floors. Leave to dry and then apply a polish formulated for these floors.

tiled floors: a damp mop is all you need

metalwork: clean to protect

metalwork Painted metalwork should first be dusted, then washed with a household cleaner. To remove rust or flaking paint, rub down with a wire brush, followed by a rust or paint remover, as necessary (see page 64).

Use a cream polish that has been formulated for stainless-steel surfaces.

A cloth soaked in malt vinegar will remove limescale and water spots from chrome-plated faucets and furniture.

natural floor coverings

Vacuum natural floor coverings thoroughly. It may be possible to remove stains by scrubbing them first with salt water and then fresh water, or use a dry-cleaning compound.

painted walls Clear the room, and place drop cloths over items that cannot be moved. At the very least, move items away from the walls to create a clear working area. Use a vacuum cleaner with a brush attachment to vacuum up as much dust as possible, in particular along chair rails and other moldings.

Next turn the electricity off if there are switches or outlets in the wall. Dilute a multipurpose household cleaner in warm water, and apply it using a large sponge. Wash one section of wall at a time, then rinse with clean water. Start at the top and work downward, so that drips can be cleaned off as you go. Don't stop midway through washing a wall, as a tidemark will form between the clean and dirty areas.

papered walls Take care when washing papered walls if you are not planning to redecorate. Vinyl wall coverings can be washed in the same way as painted walls, but don't soak the paper, or allow cleaning solution to collect in the seams. Conventional wallpaper should not be washed, but simply dusted with a soft brush or a suitable attachment on your vacuum cleaner. It may be possible to remove stains with a clean eraser or a piece of crustless white bread.

wood flooring

Wood floors with a waxed finish should be swept with a soft broom and then dry-mopped to remove dust. Sticky marks can be rubbed off with a lightly dampened cloth. If you need to remove the old wax from a wood floor, use a cloth dipped in turpentine.

To clean sealed wood floors, use a damp mop to remove dust.

woodwork Sponge down painted woodwork using a solution of dishwashing liquid, then rinse with clean water. If very dirty, use degreaser or detergent first.

woodwork: try detergent

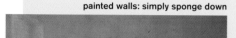
painted walls: simply sponge down

wood flooring: sweep with a soft broom first

cleaning: the furnishings

Few of us design and furnish a place completely from scratch. We cart our possessions from place to place, and we may also, unexpectedly, collect new ones. Your new home's previous occupants may, for example, leave behind some fixtures and furnishings. They may not be to your taste, but you may need to keep them. A thorough cleaning could help you to see them in a different light. You may even find you rather like them.

carpets and rugs Fitted carpets should be cleaned without overwetting the surface. Light soiling can be cleaned with a cloth and water, but heavier staining will need to be tackled with carpet shampoo or a steam-cleaning machine. Remember to place pieces of aluminum foil under any furniture legs that may touch the cleaned carpet. This stops the furniture from staining the wet textile.

Wool- and acrylic-fiber rugs can also be shampooed, and throw rugs can be handwashed in water with laundry detergent. Never attempt to wash or shampoo oriental rugs.

curtains It really is worth having large curtains professionally cleaned, as few domestic washing machines are big enough to hold them, and not many of us have the space to spread them out to

carpets: deep cleaning

dry. If you do plan to wash them at home, first loosen off any heading tapes to open pleats and gathers. Soak them in cold water to remove surface dirt, and wash them by hand if possible. Iron on the wrong side while slightly damp, then lay them on a flat surface, such as a bed, before regathering the heading tapes.

All blinds should be dusted regularly. Fabric blinds can be cleaned in the exact same way as curtains once they have been taken down and any rigid supports removed. Roman blinds, however, are best dry-cleaned to maintain their crisp appearance.

Bamboo, paper, venetian, and spongeable roller blinds can be wiped down with a weak solution of household detergent. Very greasy blinds can be cleaned in the bathtub. Lay them on an old towel to prevent them from scratching the bathtub's

curtains: best left to the experts

surface while washing, and extend them fully while drying to avoid shrinkage.

laminates

Stained laminate surfaces can be cleaned with straight dishwashing liquid, but you may need to use an abrasive cream on persistent marks.

Scratches and burn marks are impossible to remove. The best you can do is apply a melamine primer followed by gloss paint, but this is not recommended for kitchen counters and other work surfaces, as it won't stand up to constant use.

light fixtures

Before cleaning light fixtures, always make sure that they are disconnected from the electricity. Table- and floor-lamp bases can be dusted in the usual way, or cleaned using products that are suitable for use on each material.

Fabric lamp shades tend to be more fragile, and it's best to remove ingrained dirt from them with a stiff brush or a length of masking tape wrapped (sticky side out) around the hand. Some lamp shade materials,

laminates: quick and simple

including plastic and vellum, can be washed, but this is best done with a damp cloth, as immersing the shade makes the metal frame prone to rust.

light fixtures: gentleness is all

upholstery

A dusting with the vacuum cleaner, followed by the use of a specialized shampoo, goes some way to cleaning dirty upholstery. It's a good idea to test the shampoo on an inconspicuous part of the sofa first. Once the shampoo has dried thoroughly, vacuum again to remove any residue. To remove stains, use a product formulated for treating that particular problem.

Leather covers can be cleaned with a damp cloth and a proprietary leather soap.

wooden furniture

To revive stained and dirty wooden furniture, first try to work out the cause of any marks. Slight burns, water, alcohol, and heat marks (which appear white) can be rubbed away with cream metal polish, although cigarette burns respond better to fine steel wool. Once the stain has been removed, it may be necessary to use a little wood dye to correct the color. Buy this in stick form if you can find it, as it is easier to apply.

Small ink stains can be treated with absorbent cotton balls dipped in bleach – apply, then dry quickly with kitchen paper. If the stain is large, you will have to remove the wood finish first using a suitable paint or varnish remover.

design
directions

design and color

above **A wall painted in an intense blue becomes a focal point in this fresh and clean scheme, and forms the ideal backdrop to pale wood furniture.**

above **A wall painted in an intense blue becomes a focal point in this fresh and clean scheme, and forms the ideal backdrop to pale wood furniture.**

These days, even the smallest home-improvement stores offer hundreds of paint colors to choose from, so it is not surprising that we hesitate when it comes to putting together a color scheme. Most of us do have an idea of how we would like our homes to feel – when asked to describe our ideal room, descriptive phrases such as "I want somewhere warm and cozy" or "It needs to feel light and airy" trip off the tongue.

color moods

We all respond emotionally to colors, and no two people's reactions are the same. A single shade of blue will elicit comments that range from "It's so cold" to "Wow, it reminds me of the sky." Paint manufacturers have always known this – which is why they give their products such extraordinary and intriguing names. Many now organize colors into themed groups or families. These include "historical" groupings, in a variety of color combinations that are designed to suit houses of a particular period, and extensive general groupings, in which each color "family" ranges in tone from pale to dark. As the colors have been chosen to go together however you combine them, they provide an excellent foundation on which to build your scheme. Four mood-based groups are introduced below and on the following two pages.

fresh and clean

This color palette should be considered first when decorating small, dark, or north-facing rooms. The colors included in it range from sparkling pastels to zesty, tropical brights. All of these colors are very "pure," containing little or no gray or brown. This makes them a good starting point for schemes that set out to create a bold modern statement. You will also find that colors from this range suit an updated country look that uses cheerful checks and simple floral patterns.

If two or more colors are used in equal proportions – say with two walls in one color and two in another – the effect can be unsettling. A scheme from this color palette will work better if you pick a main color and give others of a similar tone smaller, supporting roles.

To see these colors at their best, light your space with halogen bulbs, which will give off clean, white light.

vibrant and stimulating

If used with confidence and care, vibrant colors are ideal for creating dramatic, highly personal schemes. This palette contains many rich, intense shades and forms a good backdrop to furnishings from those parts of the world where strong color is the norm, such as India, Mexico and the Mediterranean.

As with the "fresh and clean" palette, choose a predominant color and light the scheme with halogen bulbs.

When the more muted shades in this group are combined with cream or white, they can work well with period furnishings.

above **Vibrant colors are easier to control when they are played off against one another. It helps to retain each in a defined area, perhaps by a border of neutral painted woodwork.**

RELATED PAGES

78 getting the balance right
97 home fact file: product choices
163 summer facelift

warm and relaxing

This palette contains all those easygoing and comfortable shades that suggest mellowness and welcome. They range from cream, through yellow and peach, to amber and terra-cotta. They can be used virtually anywhere in the home, but are especially useful for cheering up dark and north-facing rooms. Most colors will happily adapt to suit the look you've chosen, although they do seem to have a natural affinity with unpainted wood, stone, and the more rustic furnishing styles. If you're not confident with color, but can't live any longer with boring white walls, this is the palette for you; it is the most forgiving of them all.

calm and neutral

Soothing and versatile, the calm and neutral group of colors is ideal for anyone who craves space, quiet, and simplicity in their home. As you might expect, it includes cream, beiges, and the many shades of white now available. However, you will also find colors such as dove gray, the paler blues and translucent lavender. All are easy to work with and gentle on the eye, and team happily with lighter woods such as ash or beech, and glass in all its guises. Pale can lack interest, but this is easily avoided by creating crisp textural contrasts. Try teaming these colors with gleaming metals, or with natural materials such as shells and grasses.

below **A relaxing color scheme is the obvious and perfect choice for more private spaces such as bathrooms. Here, warm, earthy shades help to soften the impact of hard-edged, angular or overscaled fixtures and furniture.**

fresh and clean

vibrant and stimulating

above **A calm and neutral color scheme can create the impression of space. Subtle color changes allow the eye to move easily around a room and so make it seem larger. However, textural contrasts are vital to avoid a washed-out feel.**

warm and relaxing

calm and neutral

getting the balance right

above **A mix of black-and-white geometric patterns makes a chic statement. The effect is uplifting rather than overwhelming, because one pattern – the stripe of the wallpaper – predominates. The inclusion of plain elements adds visual relief.**

If you can get dressed and make yourself look more or less presentable in the mornings, you can mix colors, textures, and patterns in your home. The principles are the same: finding the look that suits you, and creating contrasts of scale and proportion. Certain combinations work every time, whether it's the jeans and baggy sweater in your wardrobe, or blonde wood and stainless steel in the kitchen. It's important to know when to stop too: don't pile on the accessories because you feel you have to.

color and pattern

A mood board (see page 28) is a great place to start, as it will suggest possible, and perhaps contrasting, color combinations and pattern types. To work out which of these ideas will give you the finished room you want, first ask yourself what the space is to be used for. If it's for relaxing in and showing off a few prized possessions, a calm and soothing backdrop which uses colors in similar tones is ideal. On the other hand, a hive of activity, such as a family kitchen, needs to feel lively and welcoming, and a scheme based on contrasting colors will probably be more suitable.

Once you have worked out the mood, it becomes easier to incorporate pattern. You can, in fact, cram a calm room full of pattern without affecting the mood, provided all the colors are close to one another in tone.

texture

Textures make a more subtle contribution than color to a room, but are vital for creating the right feel. Shiny or smooth surfaces, such as metal and silky fabrics, reflect light and can therefore help to liven up a space. Beware though, as a room with too many shiny surfaces can feel chilly and unnerving.

At the other end of the scale, coarse or soft textures are light-absorbing, so they appear duller, albeit with more subtle color variations. They also absorb sound and feel warmer to the touch, which helps to create a sense of coziness and intimacy. Again beware, for too much softness can make a room seem airless and overdecorated.

be bold

Whatever your tastes, it often pays to be a bit daring. For example, if you want to use pattern over a large area, such as the walls, look for a design with a larger, rather than a smaller, repeat: it makes more of a statement and will look less fussy. If this sounds alarming, remember that the pattern can be broken up at regular intervals by placing

furniture in plain colors against it, or by introducing a plain floor or ceiling.

coordinated lines

Remember that many home furnishings manufacturers offer completely coordinated lines. These not only include wallpaper and fabrics in a variety of weights for upholstery and soft furnishings, but also trimmings such as braids and fringes, and accessories such as lamp shades. There are designs to suit all tastes, and nearly every line offers a choice of large-scale patterns, small all-over motifs, and matching plain colors. The best approach is to allow one design to play the starring role in a room, and use one or two others in smaller amounts.

above Textured fabrics and accessories invite you to touch them, and therefore do much to make plain or bland spaces feel more cozy and welcoming.

RELATED PAGES

28 deciding on your style
74 design and color

manipulating space

colors, such as blues and greens, appear to recede, and can be used to help to expand a space – one of the easiest ways to "raise" a low ceiling is to paint it a lighter and cooler shade than the walls.

Pattern works in complex ways to manipulate our sense of space. Our eyes move along the directions in a pattern: for example, they travel up and down vertical stripes, and in doing so help the brain to form the idea that a room is taller. By the same token, horizontal stripes can make a space seem wider. When used on the floor, diagonal or diamond-shaped patterns can also make a small room seem larger, as it takes the eye a little longer to travel in these directions.

Small-scale patterns in pale colors can help to break up and add interest to expanses of bare wall, but they need to be

above left The contrasting color of this wall marks the division between living area and kitchen in this open plan space.

above right These dark cutaway walls create a sense of privacy for a cool, light-colored bedroom.

One of the greatest things about color and, to a lesser extent, pattern and texture, is that they can be used to alter our perceptions of a space. The key point to remember is that warm colors, such as most reds, yellows, and oranges, appear to advance toward you, and can therefore be used to bring surfaces closer – you might, for example, want to "lower" a too-high ceiling or "shorten" an endless corridor. On the other hand, cool

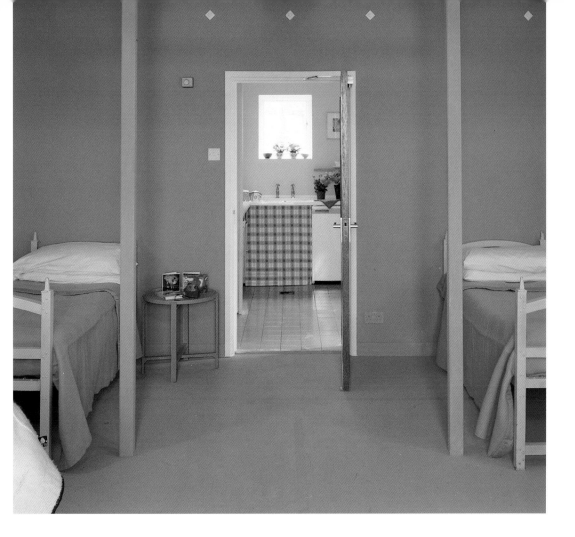

quite muted if you plan to use them all over – anything busier is likely to give the room a fussy, unsettling feel. Blanketing a room with large or complicated patterns will make it seem smaller, but a more restricted use can have the opposite effect.

Using the same floor covering in every room helps to blur the divisions between spaces, and so create a more spacious feel. Many an eyesore has been neatly camouflaged by painting it the same color as its surroundings, and creating an area of interest nearby to distract the eye.

Color and pattern can be used to divide space. For example, each activity in a multi-functional room can be defined or "zoned" by subtle changes in color and/or pattern, without destroying the overall character of the space. Or it may be possible to create a more structural "room within a room," as when you place a canopied bed in a room, or divide a space with ornamental screens.

above **Sticking to a single color for both decor and furnishings gives this potentially awkward space a womblike feel.**

RELATED PAGES

28 deciding on your style
38 space planning
74 design and color

using workhorse materials

canvas

- Firm, strong, and almost waterproof, making it ideal for outdoor use.
- Very easily painted or printed upon with fixable fabric paints.

aluminum

- Inexpensive.
- Light yet strong and corrosion-resistant.
- Available in both shiny and matte finishes.

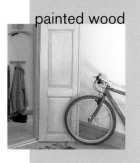

painted wood

- Limitless color and pattern possibilities.
- Easy to do yourself.
- Warm to the touch.
- Easy to clean or retouch.

linen

- Luxurious and strong, but creases easily. (Fabrics made from a blend of linen and other fibers help to avoid this problem.)

When you are decorating on a tight budget, it is more important than ever to choose materials and furnishings that will last. Cheap can often mean flimsy, and replacing items that fall to pieces after an indecently short space of time not only makes them a poor value, but also wastes a great deal of your time. Avoiding this should not pose too much of a problem, as some of the least expensive options available are also among the toughest. These include some of the oldest materials known to man, such as canvas, brick, and terra-cotta, and several with industrial origins, including plywood and stainless steel.

The description "workhorse materials" fits these perfectly because you can rely upon them to do the job well and without complaint. All need little or no maintenance, apart from standard cleaning, and although they may be functional, they are far from characterless. The colors and textures of brick and other building materials are rich and complex, while the swirls and stripes of wood grain make it one of the most satisfying of patterns.

far left **The functional approach does not have to look hard. In this bedroom, the canvas bed canopy and linen sheets soften the austere impression created by the color scheme.**

placing furniture

above **A generously sized table is a great asset in any kitchen. This design incorporates castors so it is easy to move it around. Expanding or folding tabletops also add invaluable flexibility.**

You are seldom given a free hand when it comes to arranging furniture. The shape of a room dictates where key pieces are sited; the positions of doors, windows, and other architectural features severely limit the number of places where you can put the larger items such as beds, sofas, and tables; and many of us limit the possibilities further by trying to accommodate hand-me-downs or items that don't quite fit, but are too good (or

special or useful) to throw away. When making final adjustments to the placing of furniture, a mixture of common sense and knowing what feels right usually takes care of the decision making.

As you might expect, it is best to start off by deciding where to put the largest item or items. Make sure that you can move around them easily, and that you can reach underneath them for cleaning. Wherever possible, try not to impede your view of, and access to, focal points such as windows and fireplaces. And remember to leave enough space in front of wardrobes and cabinets to enable you to open doors and drawers easily.

Working out the layout of your living room can be a bit more complicated than for other rooms, as it accommodates many activities and is most likely to be seen by other people. Comfortable seating is a must, and it needs to be grouped in ways that make it easy to be both solitary and sociable. Two sofas (if there is space) placed at an angle to one another feel friendly and flexible, while placing them directly opposite one another is more elegant but a little formal. Supplementary seating, provided by armchairs or footstools, say, also comes in useful if you regularly have friends over, as it can be used to create a more enclosed atmosphere for relaxed conversation.

Storage is the other key consideration in living spaces. It's worth remembering that it doesn't have to be pressed against the walls: it may be more useful jutting into the room so

left **A set of smaller items of furniture has creative potential. This pair of children's beds creates a pleasing sense of rhythm when positioned end to end in a room.**

that it also acts as a screen or space divider, and it can be slipped unobtrusively into furniture such as side tables or ottomans.

Whichever room you're furnishing, it's important to create contrasts of scale as well as color, texture, and pattern. The visual rhythm created by mixing larger and smaller pieces, or by boldly placing a large item in a small room, does much to give a space its character. A space in which everything is more or less the same size or height, usually waist level, feels unsettlingly lifeless and dull. This doesn't have to mean forking out for large and expensive items of furniture: a tall plant, a lamp, or a group of pictures hung high on the walls works just as well.

▸ Your basic needs are:
  a decent bed
  somewhere to sit – be it
  a couple of beanbags or
  a giant sofa
  somewhere to store clothes
  a table and chairs for eating or
  working at home
  storage for your remaining
  possessions
▸ Buy the best-quality seating
  and beds that you can afford.
  Make sure they provide good
  back support, and that you feel

choosing furniture

comfortable being in them in a variety of positions.
▸ In many small living spaces, there is only room for an L-shaped arrangement. If you can afford it, modular seating often turns out to be the best answer.
▸ Think creatively about your storage: don't blow a large chunk of your budget on built-in furniture if a modular system of rails, boxes, and shelves behind screens will do the job just as well.

designing with light

quick lighting

fixtures

- Central pendant: Try replacing the cord with a longer piece, so that the light source can be moved to where it will be most useful.
- Track or "bare wire": Spotlighting systems offer great flexibility.
- Plug-in fixtures: Include wall-mounted and clip-on types as well as floor and table lamps. The cord can be made into a feature.

bulbs

- If distracting glare is the problem, try using a crown-silvered bulb.
- Clear tungsten bulbs produce pools of light with hard edges; opal tungsten bulbs produce a softer, blurred effect.
- For a brighter, whiter, cooler light, opt for daylight bulbs.
- For an intense glow, try an amber-colored bulb.

lamp shades

- Dark colors glow softly and produce a halo effect.
- Translucent materials help to brighten the room.
- Shades with a spreading shape cast a wider pool of light.

It is difficult to overstate the importance of lighting. It determines both what we see and how we see it. Perhaps more importantly, it also fundamentally alters how we feel. Good lighting helps to keep you alert when you're working, and to unwind when you're not. It also blends into the background, to leave you free to enjoy spaces and the people within them. Bad lighting does the opposite: it competes for your attention and can leave you feeling frustrated and tense.

defining space with light

Your lighting needs vary enormously from room to room, from one time of day to another, and according to the seasons or weather. There are times when you need to see your way clearly around a space: when you're carrying stuff through a hallway or kitchen, for example, or when you need to dust and vacuum. This is made easier by providing decent levels of ambient or background light, from wall sconces perhaps, or from ceiling-mounted fixtures such as pendant lamps, eyeball spotlights, and chandeliers.

At other times, it's nicer not to see the edges of a room: when friends are gathered around a dining table, for instance, or when you want to lose yourself in a book. This is achieved by creating a pool of light that is brighter than the background, so that you are drawn into it. The lower the fixture, the smaller the pool of light and the more intimate the feel. Ideally, the light should be positioned high enough to allow light to fall where it is needed, but not so high that the bright inner surface of the shade or bulb can be seen.

When you're working, whether at a desk or in the kitchen, both the surface in front of you and your immediate surroundings must be well lit and shadow free. Atmospheric pools of light simply don't belong in work areas, because strong contrasts of light and shade are tiring for the eye and brain.

changing the mood

A flexible lighting scheme will help multi-purpose rooms to adapt to each activity. Dimmer switches are a must. They are perfect for instantly changing the mood from bright and functional to relaxing. And wherever possible, give yourself the option of being able to vary the direction and intensity of each light source. A desk lamp with a pivoting head, for example, may be used as an ambient lighting source when you're not working.

Indirect or concealed light sources make a room look flat and dull when used on their own; to feel energized and comfortable, we need to see the glow of a lit shade or the sparkle of halogen spotlights.

There is also nothing like flickering candlelight when you need to feel pampered and secure. Use candles anywhere in the house, but especially when you're in the bathtub, at the table, or outdoors on a summer evening – just don't leave them lit and unattended.

creating focal points

Good lighting shows off a room's best features and can help to play down its worst. If you have a beautiful ceiling, bouncing light upward will draw attention to it and provide attractive glare-free background illumination. Shining light downward does the opposite: it throws the ceiling into shadow and focuses attention on the lower part of the room. If you have uneven walls or ceilings, avoid shining light directly at or along them, as this highlights any defects. Try to place light sources a short distance away, so that the walls or ceiling form a softly but evenly lit background.

above **A quirky collection of lights adds interest and charm to this simply decorated space. The floor lamp in the foreground can easily be moved around. It can even be sat upon.**

lighting

Lighting serves a decorative as well as a functional purpose in interior design, and a growing awareness of its power to transform spaces means that the choice of fixtures grows ever wider. Most fit into one of the following categories.

display lighting Display lighting helps to show off pictures and favorite possessions. Picture lights, clip-on spotlights, and cabinet fixtures are just some of the options available. When lighting a picture, angle the lamp toward the image to minimize glare. Objects

floor lamps: good for corners

pendant lights: hang them in pairs or clusters for greatest impact

can be lit from the front or above to accentuate their shape and texture. If lit from behind, they create intriguing silhouettes. As well as highlighting objects or features, display lights also add attractive sparkle.

floor lamps The vertical lines of floor lamps contrast usefully with the strongly horizontal lines of most furniture. Designs range from old-fashioned standard lamps through spindly uplighters to powerful studio-style lights. They can be moved around – some are even mounted on wheels – but they need to be positioned carefully as they easily become an obstruction.

pendant lights Often to be found hanging from a single central point on a ceiling, pendant fixtures provide good background light but are hopeless at directing light to where it is most often needed, that is, at or around seated eye level. However, they can be highly decorative, especially when several are grouped together or hung in a row over a counter or table.

task lighting
Task lights should be positioned so that they keep your work area shadow-free, without exposing the bulb to the extent that it causes glare. Suitable types include desk lamps, adjustable floor lamps, clip-on fixtures and rise-and-fall pendant lights.

table lamps
Table lamps are among the most versatile fixtures available, as they provide a useful mixture of task and ambient light. A vast range of designs is available, to add a

task lights: come out of the shadows

decorative flourish to any and every scheme. Candlestick-style bases suit narrow, upright shades, while solid bases go better with wider, spreading shades.

track lighting
Lamps that are fixed to a track or wires can be removed or repositioned, which makes them useful in areas where furniture and pictures are likely to be moved around. Both tungsten and low-voltage halogen types are available. The latter add sparkle to areas of activity, such as kitchens, and spaces where you spend small

amounts of time, such as corridors or halls. However, they make living rooms and bedrooms feel hard and unrelaxing. To overcome this, fit dimmers and create pools of light lower down with plug-in lamps.

wall lamps
These can direct light upward, downward, or directly into the room through a translucent shade. They can be turned into a design feature (a row of fixtures on a long wall creates a pleasing rhythm) or, if made from plaster, painted to match the walls. To work out the best height for new fixtures, hold them about 68 inches from the floor to begin with and adjust the height from there.

table lamps: highly versatile

wall lamps: brighten up your background

incorporating technology

Modern homes are packed with electronic equipment. These days it is considered perfectly normal for a living room to contain a television, a VCR, a cable TV decoder, a stereo system, a home computer plus its printer, and, it almost goes without saying, a telephone, fax, and answering machine.

It's true that many of these pieces of equipment have been miniaturized or joined together to create multifunctional objects, but this doesn't always make them easier to use, and it doesn't solve the problem of how to incorporate them into a space that also needs to be used for relaxing and entertaining.

below **A stereo on a low table with oversized wheels entertains the eyes as well as the ears. Rows of CDs make an impressive feature.**

outlets and electrical cords

You are pretty lucky if your room contains enough outlets, in the right locations, to run all of this equipment. If you can add extra outlets, place them so that lengths of cord or cable are kept as short as possible, but make sure that you can reach them easily in order to move equipment for repairs or cleaning. Don't place them too close to the floor either, as you run the risk of creating short circuits when the floor is mopped. If you plan to use them for running computer or kitchen equipment, you could be better off placing them above the desk or counter, at waist height.

Laying extension cords with multiple outlets is a faster and cheaper alternative, but it does have serious limitations. It's easy to overload the outlet being used as the source, and if the extension cord is kept coiled up while in use, it will heat up and may be damaged. On the other hand, a loose and snaking cord easily gets tangled with other cables and can trip you if it is not kept close to the walls. Outlet adapters, which enable you to run two or more items from a single outlet, can also get dangerously hot.

Cables and cords look unsightly and have a seemingly magical ability to turn themselves into spaghetti, but there are easy ways to keep them neat and tidy. Many computer desks and stands for home entertainment equipment are constructed with channels or ducts for keeping cables concealed. This idea can be adapted for use

on any table or desk, by running cables through large cup hooks fixed underneath the back of the desktop, up a leg, or on an adjacent wall. Loose cables can also be kept together with cable ties (strong gardening ties work just as well) or a split plastic tube known as a cable organizer.

placing equipment

All electrical equipment dehumidifies the air and gives it a positive electrical charge, which contribute to an unhealthy atmosphere indoors. Houseplants and an ionizer can help to counteract this. Computer equipment can also be noisy – this can cause problems if you plan to place it in a shared or multipurpose space.

Computer and TV screens are best lit from the side to avoid annoying reflections. They should be placed at a comfortable viewing height – seated eye level is best. You may, however, have strong feelings about the extent to which electronic equipment makes its presence felt in a room. Hiding it away when it's not in use makes it easier to change the mood in multipurpose spaces. A wide variety of storage options are available, from cabinets with carousels and sliding shelves that allow you to pull the equipment out and swivel it for easy use, to carts and trolleys that can simply be wheeled out of the way.

Modern equipment has much more style than its predecessors, and many older items have a quirky retro charm, so there is no reason why you shouldn't show them off proudly. However, it's not a good idea to make them the main focal point, as they are unlikely to hold your attention for long when switched off.

above If a sense of calm is high on your list of priorities, a place to hide away the TV and other entertainment equipment is a must.

personalizing the space

The color scheme and basic furnishings of a room will make it usable, comfortable, and pleasing to the eye, but real character and atmosphere is brought to a space through the use of accessories and finishing touches.

Unless you have moved into someone else's place, or have given a professional decorator a completely free hand, or have made minimal effort because you are never at home, the look of your home is

right **If time or money is tight, remember that you don't have to decorate a room from scratch to make it yours. An adventurous sense of color, full-on use of eye-catching accessories, and temporary cover-ups for larger areas such as the floor, are guaranteed to make people forget about the original, less interesting decor.**

bound to reflect your personality. It makes a great deal of sense, therefore, to take control of this, by making conscious choices and including elements that truly reflect your tastes and interests. Indulge yourself, and show your favorite items off with pride, whether they're egg cups, textiles from an exciting foreign vacation, or your monster collection of Elvis memorabilia.

However, simply loading every surface with your stuff isn't particularly stylish or practical. It's vital to organize each group or collection, whether by color, or shape, or theme, and experiment with positioning and quantities. Think of this stage as an exercise in creating contrasts, not just of color and pattern, but also perhaps of old and new, rustic and modern, or large and small.

The simpler your scheme, the more important it becomes to get the details right. For example, if you plan to hang just one picture on the wall, make sure it stands up to being highlighted in this way, that it is hung at a height where it can be seen easily, and that it is sympathetically lit.

above A neutral color scheme is an ideal backdrop for richly patterned textiles and accessories. These have been carefully grouped to form simple, still-life arrangements, creating a sophisticated feel.

interpreting your mood board

above **Your mood board might be created by pasting magazine clippings (as suggested on page 28) or from three-dimensional objects such as these. The colors of these items have a warmth and subtlety that can be used to create a variety of looks.**

As you assess your needs and examine some of the many decorating options available, you are bound to come across decorating materials and accessories that make you instantly think, "That's it; that's exactly what I'm looking for." At times, it's possible to make a direct connection between the paint color or fabric in front of you, and an item on your mood board, because one closely matches the other. Alternatively, it may be that the color, pattern, or texture of a decorating product has a similar mood to one or more of the items on your mood board. It might be, for example, that you're inspired by pictures of certain gardens, and find yourself tempted by a wallpaper collection that isn't obviously floral, but still seems somehow right, because it's based on fresh greens and bright yellows.

Before long, you will have amassed a fair collection of products and swatches, and may even have tried out one or two paint colors on the walls. Your ideas will have begun to gel, but you may not yet have been able to make your final choices. The way to do this is to spread all the samples out on a wooden board or piece of cardboard, and ask yourself whether you like each one as much when experienced in combination with the others – after all, that's how you'll be looking at them in your finished room. You may find that the fabric you had earmarked for curtains turns out to be too heavy and dark when seen next to the wall paint color, but would look stunning as pillows. Or that while your first choice of paint shade seems a bit insipid when viewed next to all the colors, going two or three shades darker creates the perfect balance.

It won't be long before you find yourself itching to turn your ideas into a finished room scheme. Before you start, use the following pages to assemble references of your final choices for each room. If it's not practical to attach a sample of an important element, such as the style of the window treatment, represent it with photographs or drawings.

It will also be very useful to look at your samples in proportion to each other – as they

left Your aim is to translate your mood board into a generous collection of paint, paper, and fabric samples. This will enable you to see how various choices look, one against another. From this you can discard some to make your final selection.

White Pine 41-13P

Light Almond Green Lt. 41-14P

Light Almond Green 41-15M

Green Almond 41-16M

Biscay Green 41-17M

Golden Meadow 41-18D

Spr
Olly
Spring
New Lim
Tang Gre
Cool Olive
Humoresque
Golden Willow
Mayan Green

above It is very useful to
look at your product
samples, placed on a piece
of cardboard together, in
roughly the same
proportions as they will be
used. This enables you to
get an idea of the look and
feel of the end result.

will be in your finished scheme. Try this out
on a fresh piece of cardboard. If, for example,
the walls are to be painted a single color,
obtain a sample and paint an area of the
cardboard that is large enough to allow you
to place fabric and flooring swatches on top
of it. If you plan to use a particular fabric as
an accent only (as a trim for soft furnishings
perhaps), fold or roll a sample piece into a
very small strip and place it underneath the
main fabric.

Look at the assembled samples in the
relevant room during the day and at night,
and on both sunny and overcast days if
possible, to get a better idea of how the
changing light will affect the balance of
colors and textures.

Also remember to reassess your
emotional reaction to your choices. Where
appropriate, ask yourself whether you would
be happy to wake up looking at a scheme, or
walking into it at the end of a long day.

It's also a good idea to see how the
schemes for adjacent rooms relate to one
another. Too many changes in style could
give your home a disjointed feel. In smaller
homes particularly, restricting your color
range, repeating elements such as the style
of window treatment, and using the same
flooring throughout all maximize the sense of
spaciousness. It also creates flexibility. For
example, if the living room and bedroom
share certain colors, your extra dining chairs
could be used as bedside tables.

home fact file
product choices

The following home fact file pages are available for recording details of your final decorating products and samples choices. Use the "paint colors," "wallpaper," and "fabrics" boxes to stick in swatches or apply samples (along with suppliers and reference numbers). In the boxes for "tiling," "flooring," "storage," and "lighting," write down product details and attach pictures of product designs. The "detailing" box is for specifying items such as door handles and switches, and there is a spare box available for any further ideas.

hallway

paint colors

walls

reference no.
supplier

ceiling

reference no.
supplier

woodwork

reference no.
supplier

tiling

reference no.
supplier

wallpaper

reference no.
supplier

flooring

reference no.
supplier

fabrics
upholstery

reference no. _____

supplier _____

trimmings/accessories

reference no. _____

supplier _____

window treatment

reference no. _____

supplier _____

lighting
background

reference no. _____

supplier _____

task

reference no. _____

supplier _____

display

reference no. _____

supplier _____

storage
(see page 148)

reference no. _____

supplier _____

detailing

reference no. _____

supplier _____

living room

paint colors

walls

reference no.

supplier

ceiling

reference no.

supplier

woodwork

reference no.

supplier

tiling

reference no.

supplier

wallpaper

reference no.

supplier

flooring

reference no.

supplier

fabrics

upholstery

reference no. _____

supplier _____

trimmings/accessories

reference no. _____

supplier _____

window treatment

reference no. _____

supplier _____

lighting

background

reference no. _____

supplier _____

task

reference no. _____

supplier _____

display

reference no. _____

supplier _____

storage

(see page 148)

reference no. _____

supplier _____

detailing

reference no. _____

supplier _____

kitchen /dining room

paint colors

walls

reference no.

supplier

ceiling

reference no.

supplier

woodwork

reference no.

supplier

tiling

reference no.

supplier

wallpaper

reference no.

supplier

flooring

reference no.

supplier

fabrics

upholstery

reference no.

supplier

trimmings/accessories

reference no.

supplier

window treatment

reference no.

supplier

lighting

background

reference no.

supplier

task

reference no.

supplier

display

reference no.

supplier

storage

(see page 148)

reference no.

supplier

detailing

reference no.

supplier

bedroom

paint colors

walls

reference no.

supplier

ceiling

reference no.

supplier

woodwork

reference no.

supplier

tiling

reference no.

supplier

wallpaper

reference no.

supplier

flooring

reference no.

supplier

fabrics

upholstery

reference no. _____

supplier _____

trimmings/accessories

reference no. _____

supplier _____

window treatment

reference no. _____

supplier _____

lighting

background

reference no. _____

supplier _____

task

reference no. _____

supplier _____

display

reference no. _____

supplier _____

storage

(see page 148)

reference no. _____

supplier _____

detailing

reference no. _____

supplier _____

children's room

paint colors

walls

reference no. _____

supplier _____

ceiling

reference no. _____

supplier _____

woodwork

reference no. _____

supplier _____

tiling

reference no. _____

supplier _____

wallpaper

reference no. _____

supplier _____

flooring

reference no. _____

supplier _____

fabrics

upholstery

reference no.

supplier

trimmings/accessories

reference no.

supplier

window treatment

reference no.

supplier

lighting

background

reference no.

supplier

task

reference no.

supplier

display

reference no.

supplier

storage

(see page 148)

reference no.

supplier

detailing

reference no.

supplier

bathroom

paint colors

walls

reference no.

supplier

ceiling

reference no.

supplier

woodwork

reference no.

supplier

tiling

reference no.

supplier

wallpaper

reference no.

supplier

flooring

reference no.

supplier

fabrics

reference no.

supplier

lighting

background

reference no.

supplier

task

storage

(see page 148)

reference no.

supplier

reference no.

supplier

display

reference no.

supplier

reference no.

supplier

detailing

reference no.

supplier

reference no.

supplier

work/guest room

paint colors

walls

reference no.

supplier

ceiling

reference no.

supplier

woodwork

reference no.

supplier

tiling

reference no.

supplier

wallpaper

reference no.

supplier

flooring

reference no.

supplier

fabrics

upholstery

reference no.
supplier

trimmings/accessories

reference no.
supplier

window treatment

reference no.
supplier

lighting

background

reference no.
supplier

task

reference no.
supplier

display

reference no.
supplier

storage

(see page 148)

reference no.
supplier

detailing

reference no.
supplier

getting
creative

wall coverings

Choosing the right look for walls can be a daunting business. Their large surface area means you need to choose your treatment with care if you are to avoid it overwhelming the rest of your decor. The wonderful range of options available – from paint and paper to fabric, wood, and tile – doesn't make your task any easier.

An assessment of your needs will make it easier to work out which types of wall treatment are most suitable. For example, there will be practical issues to be considered, such as whether the treatment needs to wipe clean or be moisture-resistant. Your budget, skill levels, and personal tastes will also help to form a clearer picture. Once you have created a shortlist of options, the next step is to obtain samples and see how these look in situ. Allow yourself to try

paint finishes: for greater depth

one or two bolder or more adventurous options at the same time – who knows, you might even prefer them.

fabric A common way to attach fabric to a wall is to apply it directly, which is easiest with stiff, medium, or heavyweight fabrics, such as canvas or felt. The fabric can be glued on (the adhesive should be applied to the wall rather than the fabric) or stapled into place. Alternatively, and traditionally, fabric is hung on battens or shirred onto a track or stretched wires. This suits lighter fabrics such as cottons and muslins. Some fabrics, including silk and burlap, are available backed with paper and can be hung like wallpaper. However, the seams are usually difficult to disguise.

paint finishes, flat The most versatile and budget-friendly of all decorating materials, paint is also one of the easiest to work with and reassuringly simple to cover up if things should go wrong. The range of types available is enormous, ranging from standard water- or oil-based formulations, through old-fashioned recipes such as distemper, to paints that have been engineered to cover walls literally in one coat, or remain impervious to water. The choice of colors is effectively limitless –

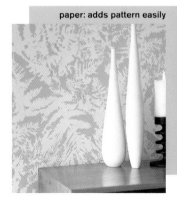

paper: adds pattern easily

many larger stores can match paint colors exactly to a supplied swatch of fabric, paper, or other material with the use of a computer-controlled spectrometer.

paint finishes, layered and textured Simple layered paint effects such as ragging and sponging are an easy yet effective way to give walls a subtly patterned feel. If you're a novice decorator, it's best to use similar colors for each layer, as this helps to disguise mistakes and patchiness. Layering paints and glazes is a time-consuming but satisfying process, as it can produce finishes with an unbelievable depth and subtlety. Textured paints are useful for covering up small cracks and imperfections. The latest examples are subtler in appearance than their predecessors, but both create a rough surface that is difficult to clean and a nightmare to remove.

paneling Cladding with tongue-and-groove paneling is a fashionable and practical way to cover up uneven walls. As the panels are fixed to battens, a gap is created between them and the wall behind, so that they also act as an excellent heat and noise insulator. Inexpensive softwoods such as pine or man-made boards such as MDF are usually used to manufacture such paneling, and their appearance is greatly improved by painting or staining. If a water-resistant finish is used, tongue-and-groove can also be used in wet areas such as bathrooms.

paneling: tough and insulating

plaster finishes Although they are never the simplest or cheapest options, plaster finishes have a depth of color that simply cannot be matched by surface effects such as paint. Like traditional frescoes (from which they are

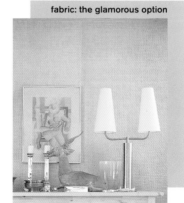
fabric: the glamorous option

descended), they consist of a thin layer of white plaster that has been tinted with pigments. The plaster can also be mixed with ground materials, such as marble, so that it shimmers and catches the light. This is not an easy technique to learn, and application is best left to specialist craftsmen.

special papers Woodchip, foamed polyethylene, and embossed papers add texture to walls, are tougher than conventional papers, and are designed to be painted over. They can also be used to cover small imperfections in walls and ceilings. Their popularity is on the wane, partly because they have an old-fashioned feel, but also because they can be unpleasant to touch.

tiles The range of ceramic tiles available is so great that it seems a

shame to limit their use to kitchens and bathrooms. Their hard-wearing surface is ideal for hallways, but they can also be useful wherever a tough but good-looking finish is required. Tile sizes range from tiny mosaics to large 2-ft x 1-ft panels. It's worth remembering that as tiles get smaller, the number of gaps for grouting gets larger.

wallpaper Wallpapers are perfect for creating a patterned or textured backdrop, and they can be very useful when you need to disguise poor proportions or uneven wall surfaces. The most commonly available types are standard and vinyl. The former are thin and tear easily, especially when dampened with paste. The latter are easier to hang and remove, especially if bought in a ready-pasted form, but the top vinyl layer can have a cheap-looking sheen when seen over large areas.

tiles: glossy and hard-wearing

painting glossy walls

Walls that glow richly make a room look glamorous, but painting them with gloss paint is not the best way to achieve this. The best way to create glossy surfaces with depth and subtlety is to build up layers of color and varnish. For an even richer look, use tinted varnish, as here.

tools • clean rag or sponge • batten • spirit level • paint bucket • good-quality, clean 3- or 4-inch paintbrush

materials • paint • thin cardboard for template • pencil • low-tack masking tape • clear polyurethane varnish (1 quart should be enough for a 9-ft x 12-ft room) • turpentine • artists' oil paint

1   Paint the walls in your chosen base color. Ordinary latex paint is fine for this. Leave the paint to dry, and then wipe down thoroughly with a clean rag or sponge to remove as much dust as possible.

2   Make a template from thin cardboard. A diamond shape was used here, but other geometric forms work just as well. If necessary, lightly draw a horizontal guideline at the base of the walls with a batten, spirit level, and pencil.

4

Fix the template lightly to the walls using low-tack masking tape, and mask off the pattern. Do not press the masking tape down too hard, as this can damage the base coat when it is removed.

3 Mix roughly three parts of clear varnish with one part of turpentine in a paint bucket. Dissolve a blob of artists' oil paint in a little turpentine, then add this to the diluted varnish. It is best to use an oil paint color that complements the base coat, as the end result is more difficult to control with very different colors. The pattern can be made more obvious by adding more oil paint to the varnish to make the tint stronger.

4 Apply the tinted varnish using light and even brush strokes, and leave to dry until hard. This can take a few days. Repeat if necessary. When the varnish is completely dry, carefully remove the masking tape. Allowing the varnish to dry before you do this will give the pattern a cleaner edge.

glossy furniture finish

A high-gloss paint finish looks just as good on furniture. It is reasonably easy to achieve, as long as your working environment can be kept dust-free, and your surface is smooth to begin with. This is not a good technique for covering up scratches.

First brush an oil-based primer over the surface, and allow it to dry. Rub the surface smooth with fine sandpaper. Then remove all traces of dirt with clean, damp rags. Next, with a clean brush, apply an even layer of gloss paint, and leave it to dry, then rub down and clean as before. Repeat at least once more. Finally, apply the top coat and leave to dry.

rubber-stamping walls

One of the easiest, fastest, and yet oldest ways to add pattern to walls is to stamp them with a repeated motif. You can make your own stamp – simple geometric shapes such as circles and squares give the best results – but you will get sharper results with a ready-made stamp.

tools • plumb line • spirit level • straight edge or batten • paint tray or saucer • paint mixing stick or spatula • rubber stamp • paint roller (foam type) • damp sponge

materials • chalk or pencil • paint (artists' acrylic paints work especially well) • sheet of paper or cardboard

1 Measure and mark out the area to be stamped, using a plumb line to establish vertical guidelines for your stamped pattern. Mark the position of each motif using chalk or a pencil. If you want the motifs to form a regular grid pattern, you will also need to draw horizontal guidelines. To do this, use a spirit level resting on a batten or straight edge.

2 Pour a little paint into a paint tray, or squeeze artists' acrylic paint onto a saucer.

more uses for your rubber stamp

It is just as easy to stamp onto fabric, tabletops, and other flat surfaces. You can also stamp accessories such as lamp shades, providing you can hold them still while you press on the stamp.

You can make your own stamp by cutting into the surface of a close-textured household sponge. However, prints from homemade stamps will tend to give a "softer," more blurred effect.

If using paint from a tube, flatten it slightly with a mixing stick or spatula. Apply a coat of paint to the stamp using the foam roller (this is neater and cleaner than pressing the stamp into the paint and ensures that you get an even coverage of paint over the stamp).

3 Test your stamp on a sheet of paper or cardboard. If the print looks clear with crisp edges, you know you have the right amount of paint on the stamp.

4 Now stamp the design onto the wall. Work from the top downward, if possible, as this reduces the chances of smearing the wet prints. Apply more paint to the stamp as necessary. Do not worry if some of the prints look less bright or sharp than the others; this is inevitable when you print by hand and is one of stamping's attractions.

If you need to remove a blurred or smudged print, use a damp sponge and wipe the image off the wall immediately. Do this very carefully to avoid ruining any other prints. When you have finished, clean the stamp with soapy water.

creative wallpapering

3

A personal computer can help you transform your interior. This contemporary mural of metal flooring was enlarged on the computer to give it a more abstract feel. When the printouts were pasted together, we were left with a sophisticated, three-dimensional pattern.

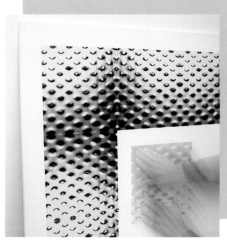

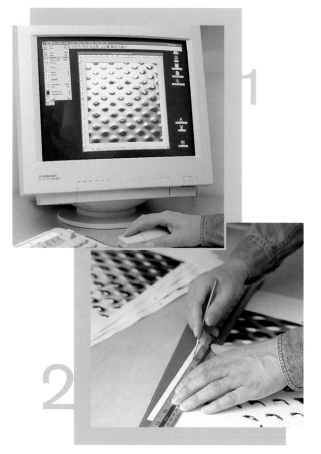

1

2

tools • computer with graphics software • scalpel • steel rule • cutting mat • wallpaper seam roller • 3- or 4-inch paintbrush

materials • your chosen image (on disk or with access to a scanner) • 8½ x 11-inch paper • medium-density fiberboard (MDF) • wallpaper paste • clear polyurethane varnish

1 Find your image. Copyright- and royalty-free images can often be found on the CDs given away with computer magazines. If you use other images, be sure to obtain any copyright permission.

Load the image onto your Mac or PC. If you have graphics software, you can then enlarge, recolor, reverse, or cut and paste elements. Once you are happy with the result, print out as many sheets as you need. You can paste paper straight on to the wall or create a mural on fiberboard as we have done here.

computer collage

If you have access to a scanner, as well as a computer, you can use your own photographs in your wallpaper designs. Creating a bank of pictures in a digitized format is a great way to store souvenirs and memories, and it means that you can blend and overlay images without having to worry about destroying the original. Once you get the hang of the technology, all kinds of effects become possible.

2 On a cutting mat, use a scalpel and steel rule to trim off any borders to the picture on each sheet. Our mural used 16 sheets of 8½ x 11-inch paper (trimmed). We created two slightly different 8½ x 11-inch paper images by using the computer's graphics package to flip the original design and create its own mirror image. These were glued down alternately on the board, to create the pattern shown.

3 Cut a sheet of MDF to the size of your completed design plus an additional allowance for a border all around. Paint the border area of the board and, when dry, glue each sheet in place using wallpaper paste. You may want to use a seam roller to push out any air bubbles.

4 Finally, give the mural a couple of coats of polyurethane varnish. As well as protecting the paper, this gives a lustrous, reflective finish. You can also tint the varnish with a little artists' oil paint, so as to add another layer of color.

creative tiling

Mosaic tiling always adds a touch of handcrafted luxury to a bathroom or kitchen. As well as providing you with a tough, water-resistant, and easy-to-clean surface where it is most needed, it's a great way to add color and pattern.

tools • coarse sandpaper • panel pins or adhesive • safety goggles • old sheet or towel • hammer • tile cutter • tile nippers • grease pencil • tile adhesive spreader • grout spreader • clean rags

materials • wood or MDF beading • pencil and large sheet of scrap paper • tiles (buy about 10 percent more than for the area you are decorating, to allow for waste) • tile adhesive • grout

1 Ensure that the walls are smooth and clean. If you plan to tile over a gloss-painted surface, sand it first with coarse sandpaper.

Establish the area to be tiled, and pin or glue wood or MDF beading around the edges to create a border. Draw out the dimensions of the area on a sheet of scrap paper. Put on safety goggles, wrap the tiles in an old sheet or towel, smash them with a hammer, and pick out the cleanly broken pieces. Arrange these within

the lines on your paper to form your design. Alternatively, draw out a design and trim the pieces to fit accordingly.

2 Shape the tiles using a tile cutter and nippers. If it helps, sketch out the shape to be cut on the surface of the tile using a grease pencil. Place the cut tiles over the design you have drawn out on paper until the entire area has been covered.

3 Apply tile adhesive to the wall, over a small area at a time, using a notched spreader. Position each piece of tile according to your design and press into place. Let dry.

4 Use a spreader to fill all the cracks with grout (use waterproof grout where necessary). Remove any excess with a clean, damp cloth, and let dry. If you are tiling a shower area, let grout harden completely (up to four days) before using. When dry, buff up the tiles with a clean, dry coarse cloth, such as burlap.

tiling furniture

Small, flat surfaces such as tabletops and cupboard door panels are a great place to show off your mosaic tiling skills, as relatively small amounts of tiles are needed, and even the simplest design makes them look special.

If you are going to undertake this, remember that the edges are the most vulnerable part of any tiled surface, so you should create a protective edging for your design, either by using wood or MDF beading. Alternatively, lay the tiles on a slightly recessed surface, so that your design sits flush with its surroundings.

fabric paneling

If you ache to use beautiful fabrics in a room, but expensive curtains are not an option, why not hang a smaller amount of fabric on the wall? Suspend floaty fabrics as simple banners; frame fine weaves and embroidery like pictures; or hang rugs and throws from battens.

tools • pencil • metal tape measure • batten and spirit level • plumb line • drill • fabric pins • sewing machine • screwdriver

materials • 4 pad eyes, with a D-shaped loop welded on and two holes for screwing to the wall (available from boating supply stores) • screws • fabric • 1/16-inch stiff construction wire with a 3/16-inch tensioner at one end and hard eyes at both

1 Decide on the length and width of your banners. Mark the position of one pad eye on the wall. Using a batten and spirit level, lightly draw a horizontal line to establish the position of the second pad eye.

Next, mark the positions of the lower pad eyes. Use a plumb line to ensure that these line up with the upper pad eyes and measure the distance between both pairs to check that they are equal. Drill the screw holes for the pad eyes.

fast ways to hang fabric

Covering walls with thick fabric makes sense if the wall surface is poor, or if you need extra insulation. Hem any raw edges, then punch large eyelets at regular intervals along the top edge of each length. Either hang them on hooks fixed to the wall, or thread onto a tensioned wire as shown at left. Alternatively, screw battens along the top and bottom edges of the walls, and staple on the fabric.

2 Lay your fabric on a flat surface, and measure out the length needed. Add 2 x 3 inches (total 6 inches) to this to allow for hemming. Cut the fabric to length. Fold over 3 inches at each end, then fold this strip in on itself to create a 1½-inch-wide channel. Pin and sew into place. If using a sewing machine, make sure it is correctly tensioned for the type of fabric being sewn.

3 Our wire was made up to order by a yacht chandler. This way you can specify the measurements that you require, and they will make up each length of wire complete with tensioner and pad eyes in place. Simpler versions are available from DIY stores. Screw the pad eye attached to the end of the wire without the tensioner to the wall, then thread the other end of the wire and tensioner through the fabric channel as shown.

4 Loosen the thread in the tensioner and then screw the pad eye to the wall. Once in place, tighten the thread in the tensioner until the fabric lies flat and taut.

floor surfaces

Whether you opt for a richly colored carpet or pale wood strip, your floor treatment makes an excellent, and time-honored, starting point for a decorative scheme. Like your wall treatment, it covers a large surface area, and therefore acts as a useful backdrop. The color and pattern can also help to alter the room's proportions. Light colors, small patterns, and plain surfaces make a space feel airier, while laying tiles on the diagonal will appear to push the walls outward, making a small room feel larger. Conversely, dark colors and strong patterns can help to shrink a space: you might, for example, use a boldly patterned rug to anchor and draw together a varied group of furniture.

The floor treatment is often the single most expensive element in a scheme, so it may well need to last for several years. There are practical considerations too: it needs to be easy to clean, comfortable to walk upon, and perhaps soft enough to cushion a child's fall.

carpet The softest of all the flooring options, carpets can be fitted to the contours of a room or loose-laid to cover part of the floor. The way they are made determines their character to a large extent; tufted examples are

springier underfoot, while flat-weave rugs have a pleasingly ribbed or nubbly feel. Abstract and free-form designs are easier to reproduce on tufted carpets, but the designs on flat-weave rugs often have a crisper, more defined feel.

concrete Although it is more often used as a base for other floor coverings, concrete also makes a stylish, practical floor treatment in its own right. A smooth and level floor can be painted easily. The most common problems associated with old concrete floors are cracking and holes – which should be filled with mortar – and places where old carpet adhesive has dried on. This can be removed with a special solvent.

linoleum and vinyl Available in both sheet and tile form, linoleum and vinyl feel warm and flexible underfoot,

linoleum: easily customized

matting: fragrant and tactile

are easy to lay, and will last for years if properly looked after. Linoleum is one of the most environmentally friendly decorating materials available, as it is made from renewable natural resources such as linseed oil and burlap. However, vinyls are available in a wider range of designs.

matting Natural floor coverings, as mattings are often known, are made from plant fibers such as coir, jute, and sea grass. These are plaited and woven to form surfaces with strongly defined textures. They are laid much like carpet and are often a good alternative to it, especially if you're trying to create a more rustic feel.

rubber As it is easy to clean, stable, and very hard-wearing, rubber flooring is most commonly found in commercial and industrial spaces. It is, however, well worth considering if your floor needs to be both tough and flexible; it is impossible to stain and is hardly affected even by sharp objects and cigarette burns.

tiles: tough and wipe clean

tiles Ceramic, terra-cotta, and quarry are the most popular tile options for floors. All of these are made from clay, but they look very different, and their

stained wood: luxurious yet practical

water resistance varies. Terra-cotta and quarry tiles have a less uniform appearance than ceramic tiles, which gives them a rustic feel. They are also thicker, which can make them more difficult to lay.

wood Most houses and apartments built before the 1950s have wooden floors. In some parts of the world, these are likely to consist of softwood planks set on joists. Elsewhere, parquet or wood-block floors, laid in attractive patterns, are the norm. Modern wood floors have tongue-and-groove edges, which eliminate drafts from under the floor, and help to disguise shrinkage and movement of the planks. They can be made from solid wood or laminated: several layers of man-made board topped by a thin layer of real wood. Laminate is cheaper, often more stable, and much faster to lay.

Solid wood and thicker laminated floors can be sanded down and protected with layers of varnish, or colored with paints or stains. A wide variety of effects is possible, from the glossy and smooth look created by paint, to treatments that highlight the natural texture and pattern of wood, such as liming.

sealed floorboards: a warm backdrop

quick cover-ups

▶ Large rugs and mats can be bought cheaply and are invaluable for covering up ugly or cold floor coverings. Alternatively, stitch together narrow runners to create a larger rug.

▶ It may be possible to dye a fitted carpet made from natural fibers such as wool. This job is best left to specialists, however, as it's difficult to get an even color.

▶ Plywood and hardboard "tiles" (see page 128) provide a fast and cheap solution to the problem of laying a new floor.

▶ Now available in a wider variety of colors and textures, carpet tiles are easy to lay, and two or more shades can be combined to create patterned areas (see page 130).

fixing wooden floor panels

Real wood floors look wonderful, are easy to look after, and age beautifully, but they are seldom affordable. However, it is possible to get the look and feel of real wood on a budget by using sheets of plywood to create this simple but stylish checkerboard effect.

tools • ripsaw • chalk line or string • hammer • sturdy craft knife • nail punch • large paintbrush

materials • hardboard to cover your floor area • small panel pins • 3/8-inch-thick plywood (when cut into tiles, ours measured 1 ft x 1 ft. Each tile should be tongued on two adjacent sides, and grooved on the remaining two.) • satin varnish

1 Cover the floor with sheets of hardboard to provide a flat working surface. These should have been brushed with water on the rough side, stacked flat, and left to dry for several hours beforehand. They should be laid in large panels, rough side down, with the joints staggered. Hardboard can be cut with a ripsaw if necessary. Secure the sheets with panel pins.

2 Find the center point of your floor. To do this, measure the midpoint along two

different effects

Wood stains and varnishes can be tinted with oil paint to create richer or more unusual effects. If your floorboards have an unattractive yellow tinge, try staining them a darker color using wood stain or tinted wax. You can then seal the surface with varnish that has been tinted with black artists' oil paint. To do this, dissolve a blob of oil paint in a little turpentine, and add this mixture to the varnish.

opposite walls. Either draw a chalk line or fix a taut length of string between these points. Repeat this process with the other two walls. Where the two lines cross is your center point. You can now adjust this point so that it lines up with the center of a feature such as a fireplace.

Mark the center of the first plywood tile, and place it on your center point. Before fixing it in place, lay down several rows of tiles as a "dry run", from the center of the room outwards, to check that the tiles at the edges of the room do not have to be cut into awkward slivers. Adjust as necessary.

3 Using panel pins, nail each tile down by hammering the pins at a 45° angle through the tongued sides. Drive the pins below the surface with a nail punch so that the tiles can be slotted together. Lay the tiles so that the grain on each one is at right angles to that of its neighbor.

4 Using a large brush, apply two to three coats of satin varnish. A tougher varnish will need to be used in heavy traffic areas.

laying carpet tiles

Carpet tiles are much easier to lay than floor coverings that are sold off the roll, as they are quickly maneuvered into place and trimmed to size. We took advantage of this to create a custom-designed fitted carpet with a built-in central pattern or "rug."

tools • ripsaw • chalk line or string • hammer • metal rule • cutting mat • steel rule • sturdy craft knife

materials • hardboard to cover your floor area • panel pins • square carpet tiles • carpet adhesive • double-sided carpet-to-floor tape • strong, wide (gaffer) tape

1 Cover your floor with sheets of hardboard and find the center point of your floor, as explained on pages 128–129. You may want to adjust this point so that it lines up with the center of a feature such as a fireplace or a bay window. This will make your "rug" appear more central in the room.

Glue your first carpet tile down on the center point with carpet adhesive. This tile needs to be glued down, as all the others are tightly butted up to it. It is also a good idea to

tape every third row of tiles down with double-sided carpet-to-floor tape for a secure fit.

2 Make your patterned tiles. First mark the cutting lines on the reverse side of each tile, and then cut cleanly along each one using a steel rule and sharp craft knife.

To make the pattern shown here, we cut variously colored 16-inch x 16-inch tiles each into sixteen equal strips, each measuring 2 inches x 8 inches. The strips were then mixed up to create the striped pattern shown.

3 To assemble each patterned tile, butt two lots of eight strips tightly up to one another, and stick them together with strong, wide tape. These can now be placed on the floor in the same way as the whole tiles.

4 To cut border tiles, slide an uncut tile upside down under the nearest whole tile, as shown, and mark along the edge to form a cutting line. This helps to ensure a tight fit. Cut as before.

another idea

Carpet tiles are especially suitable for rooms that get dirty quickly and often. The short pile makes it easier to clean them, and if an area becomes worn or stained, you only have to replace the damaged squares.

The approach taken here can easily be adapted to suit the size and shape of your room. Try using several colors of tile to create a cheerful harlequin effect in a kitchen or child's room. Or bring grandeur to your hallway by laying tiles in two strongly contrasting colors – one light, the other dark in tone – in a checkerboard pattern.

window and door solutions

Attractive windows and doors are real assets, as they add both character and architectural detail to a room. They say much about the age and style of your building (and in the case of external windows, really should be faithful to these). They help to create privacy, but also play a large part in determining whether a room is enjoyable to use. A badly positioned door, for example, wastes space, makes it difficult to move around, and can frustrate your efforts to create a workable furniture layout. And few of us would willingly occupy a windowless room for long.

Despite their importance, we are often boringly predictable in the way we decorate doors and windows. We paint them a neutral color, such as white, or cover them up with net curtains, and expect them to recede into the background. However, there are many more ways to turn them, without difficulty, into eye-catching features. A few ways to get the best out of your windows and doors are outlined here and on the following pages.

blinds Although they are available in a variety of styles and materials, blinds generally have a simpler and more architectural feel than curtains, as they sit neatly on or within a window frame. They are less likely to overwhelm small windows, and when several are used to dress a large window area, they provide greater flexibility. To let in as much daylight as possible, choose a type that can be pulled clear of the window pane.

curtains and sheers

Nothing softens the lines of a bare or underfurnished room as effectively as a

curtains: for softness

set of curtains. The design possibilities are limitless, although your choice should take factors such as the shape of the window, the overall look of the room, and, of course, your budget into consideration (large amounts of fabric are needed for even the simplest curtain treatments).

As well as choosing the right fabric, it's important to consider the hanging method (rods are more decorative, but tracks are neater, as long as they can be concealed). Sill-length curtains look more informal than full length, but this may not be appropriate in rooms with large or grand windows. Remember also that trimmings, linings, and accessories can dramatically alter the final look, and cost, of your curtains.

roller blinds: cutouts create patterns of light

Like other window treatments, curtains also serve several practical purposes: as well as creating privacy and excluding drafts, they help to keep the heat in during cold weather and can be used to stop rooms from overheating in the summer.

The pattern of pleats at the top of a curtain is known as the heading. It affects how much fabric will be required, and how it falls when the curtains are closed. A variety of styles can be created using ready-made heading tapes. For a more casual feel, curtains can be simply gathered onto a rod using loops, ties, a casing, or eyelets.

slatted blinds: adaptable

replace it with a decorative curtain or fabric panel?

shutters: add architectural interest

door openings If a door that links two spaces is unnecessary – as is often the case with, say, adjacent living and dining areas – why not

shutters Shutters provide a practical and fuss-free alternative to blinds and curtains. They are particularly good at cutting out strong sunlight and noise, and if they can be securely fastened, they offer added security. Traditional examples are paneled or louvered, but examples made from painted board work just as well.

solid and glazed doors

Whether paneled or flat, solid doors provide a sturdy and effective barrier (as long as they are fitted properly)

against noise and drafts. They are also the most sensible option if locks and bolts are being used. Glazed or semi-glazed doors may be a better bet for internal doors, as they help to bring light into darker areas, such as hallways. Use frosted or patterned glass for greater privacy.

sliding and folding doors

Conventional doors take up considerable amounts of floor and wall space, so sliding and folding doors are well worth considering for small and narrow rooms. They also allow spaces to flow into one another. You could, for example, use them to alternately open up and screen off the kitchen from your living space, or to hide working clutter in a study-bedroom.

sliding doors: space-saving

creating privacy

below **Window cover-ups need not be complicated or expensive. This length of light, plain fabric is simply pinned into place at each corner.**

Large expanses of permanently bare window are simply not a viable option for most town or city dwellers. The idea that you can be watched while inside your home produces an acute sense of discomfort in most people, and there are times, such as late at night or

most obvious candidates, closely followed by home offices and bedrooms. It's worth remembering that high levels of external noise and drafts can also invade your privacy; it may be necessary to insulate against these too.

There may be instances, when a window faces into a dingy light well or onto an eyesore, when you will feel the need to completely shut out the view.

Dressing windows with sheer fabrics such as voile, lace, and muslin is a popular and effective way to create privacy. These fabrics can be used to veil the window rather than shut out all the light, and work especially well when either generous quantities of fabric are used, to create a glamorous and ethereal feel, or when the fabric is tailored to form crisp, flat panels. Colored sheers subtly tint light as it passes through, making them ideal for

right **Your choice of screening should also work on a practical level. Shower curtain fabric is ideal for a window in a bath area.**

during bad weather, when it is positively comforting to shut out the rest of the world.

If you share your home or have visitors, it is also important to give certain rooms a greater feeling of privacy. Bathrooms are the

- A paneled, freestanding screen makes a good temporary cover-up for bare windows. However, it could take up precious floor space and may be difficult to maneuver.
- Prefinished lengths of fabric such as blankets, throws, and sarees make great no-sew curtains. Simply hang from a rod with curtain clips, or fix in place with staples or pins.
- Alternatively, drape a piece of fabric that is double the length required over a rod or pole. With lighter fabrics it may be necessary to weight the ends with a heavier fabric or trimming.
- To partially cover a window, fix pegs or rings to the upper corners of a window frame, and attach a sheet of fabric by tying on the corners.

warming up cold, north-facing rooms. And there's no need to scour the shops for the right color, as fabrics made from natural yarns are extremely easy to dye at home.

For greater privacy, clear glass can be replaced with an opaque or patterned design, or at little expense you can mimic the appearance of these. Frosted self-adhesive plastic sheets can be used to cover an entire pane of clear glass, or be cut into patterns or motifs for a more decorative look. It is also possible to frost glass by stippling on a mixture of white oil paint and varnish, in equal parts. This works best when areas of glass are masked off first to create a pattern, as this helps to disguise any possible unevenness in the paintwork.

If you need a degree of adjustability in your screening, louvered blinds, shutters, or a pull-up roller blind could be the answer. The slats of the former can be angled to provide both privacy and a partial view of the outside, while the latter allows the lower portion of a window to be screened off, while light floods in through the upper part.

above **Fixing lengths of twisted colored ribbon over a window is a simple yet effective way to create privacy without shutting out the view. The ribbons form constantly changing patterns when they are ruffled by a breeze.**

customizing doors and windows

above **Colored glass will turn a dull window into something special and divert attention away from a depressing view. There is no need to go as far as installing new panes of glass: the effect can also be achieved by using colored plastic films, glass paint, or sheets of tissue or rice paper.**

Replacing doors and windows is not always a viable option; you are more likely to have to make the most of what you've got.

Plain frames can benefit greatly from the addition of moldings. A variety of traditional designs are available, or you could adopt a theatrical approach by cutting extravagant shapes out of medium-density fiberboard.

Attention will be drawn to doors and windows if you paint them a contrasting color to the walls. However, if a door doesn't fit well into its frame, or if several doors open into one room, it may be more desirable to lessen their impact. The easiest way to do this is to paint them to match their surroundings.

Doors make an ideal backdrop for paint effects and murals. They can also be livened up by covering them with a thin sheet of metal, with glued-on fabric (for best results, choose something stiff, like felt), or self-adhesive plastic.

Windows can be livened up in a much greater number of ways with curtains and blinds. The choice of styles and materials is huge, and you should base your choice not just on personal taste, but also on practical considerations such as the size, style, and operating mechanism of the window; the room's function; and the need for privacy.

Like other hardware, such as switch plates or outlets, door and window handles are design details that are repeated in every room, so it makes sense for them to be the same throughout your home. This will instantly create a more finished, stylish look. However, good hardware is seldom cheap. If your budget won't stretch to paying for replacements, your option is to give existing handles a good cleaning, and/or paint them with enamel paints (do this carefully to avoid clogging up moving parts).

The glass in doors and windows can also be painted to add character. This works best on small panes, as the thinness of the paint produces a streaky effect over larger areas.

Lastly, don't overlook the possibilities for display in these areas. Objects can be propped on a windowsill, or hung from a pole or hooks in a window recess. Even doors can be pressed into service: a hook or two provides useful storage, or they can be used as a place to fix bulletin boards, pictures, and mirrors.

below There is no need to be limited by conventional window coverings. These lightweight frames are covered with translucent fabric and mounted on a track to create an elegant cross between shutters and curtains. This would need to be custom-made, but as it is almost a work of art, it is an option worth considering.

above Doors have long been used to display craftsmanship of the highest order, often in the form of paneling and carving. This etched steel door is a modern interpretation of this idea. The effect could also be created by hand-drawing or stenciling onto a metallic painted surface.

painting fabric blinds

Fabric paints and pens make it easy to customize plain curtains and blinds. The most suitable fabrics for this type of treatment are those with a smooth finish, such as cotton or calico. Silk and velvet can also be used, but colors do tend to "bleed" slightly more on these.

tools • artists' or stenciling paintbrushes • iron • sewing kit • staple gun, or hammer and tacks

materials • fabric • fabric stiffener • tailors' chalk • fabric paints or pens • roller blind kit

1 If you intend to turn your fabric into a roller blind, as here, you will need to stiffen it first. To do this, use a fabric stiffener and follow the manufacturer's instructions.

Next, lay the fabric on a flat surface, and mark out your design. Simple geometric designs are easiest to achieve. Draw your design onto the fabric using tailors' chalk if possible. This will produce marks that are light enough to be painted over easily.

2 If using fabric paints, pour a little into a saucer, and fill in the design using a fine artists' brush. Alternatively, if you are planning

other fabric painting methods

Latex, acrylic, and spray paints also give great results on fabric. Spray paints produce even layers of color that can be built up to produce graduated effects, and they can also be used in conjunction with masking tape to produce crisp lines and geometric forms. When using other kinds of paint, try stippling or ragging the paint onto the fabric for different effects.

to mix paints to create your own color, make sure that you mix enough for the whole design at one time (if you run out halfway, it is unlikely that you will be able to mix exactly the same color again). Work from the furthest point toward you to reduce the risk of smudging wet paint. When finished, let the paint dry. If you are using more than one color, let each one dry before applying the next.

3 Fix your design with a hot iron, or according to the fabric paint manufacturer's instructions (always read these before starting, as they can vary between paints). Iron the reverse side of the fabric to prevent damaging the painted pattern.

4 Then use your fabric to make the roller blind. First, trim and hem the fabric to prevent fraying and to give a more professional finish; then attach it to the roller blind. We found it easiest to attach the fabric to the roller with a staple gun (as shown here), but a hammer and tacks can be used if you prefer.

making space work harder

As homes get smaller, every available square foot has to work even harder. Today, nearly every room serves more than one purpose, and the way they are decorated and furnished therefore needs to accommodate this.

flexible furniture

One of the key requirements in any multipurpose space is that it should be possible to move some of the furniture around. For example, wheeled items can be moved to where they are needed, or out of the way. Folding and stacking pieces also help to free up precious space when not in use. Furniture that can genuinely be used for more than one purpose is also invaluable: certainly, no home should be without a couple of sturdy stools, as they can be used as seats or as side tables. Three or four small tables can also be placed together to create a larger one.

zoning

It also helps to increase the sense of space if different activities occupy clearly defined zones. This can be achieved by physically dividing the space, either with low walls or pieces of furniture: for example, you could place the bed behind a screen in a study-bedroom, or hide kitchen mess

right **A trio of cabinets makes the most of available wall space and allows the areas between them to be used for display. Stacking chairs are ideal when space is limited.**

behind a low wall that doubles as a breakfast counter in an open-plan living room.

defining space with color

Activity zones can also be suggested by changes in decor. A richly colored wall or painting helps to anchor items of furniture that are placed nearby. The same thing happens when we arrange seating around a rug in a living or dining area. An advantage of this approach is that it needn't be permanent. The rug can be rolled away, and the painting hung elsewhere, when you feel like a change.

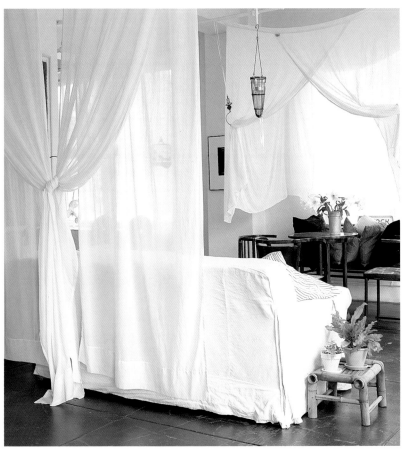

left **Placing a sofa in the center of a room can help to create a more dynamic layout, but you may feel more exposed here. To counteract this, simply place some form of screening behind the sofa.**

below **Industrial materials give a paneled screen an up-to-date feel.**

putting things away

If a multipurpose space is to be used intensively, it must be easy to move around in. To ensure this, the floors need to be kept as clear as possible, and you will need excellent storage systems. It is vital, for example, to be able to put away work clutter before a room can be used for relaxing in. One could also argue that keeping the level of unnecessary visual distractions (in other words, mess) to a minimum makes a room feel larger, as well as more soothing. This is not to say that we should all aspire to living like medieval monks. One of the greatest things about having well-planned storage is that it allows you to choose what to leave on display – you only have to look at those items that give you pleasure.

RELATED PAGES

38 space planning
84 placing furniture
142 storage

storage

Whether grand or humble, traditional or modern, all forms of storage are variations on the idea of a shelf, a hook, or a box. Sometimes, of course, they can be a combination of the three. A kitchen drawer unit, for example, is a series of boxes placed on top of one another surmounted by a shelf – also known as the countertop.

built-in storage This makes good use of limited and awkward spaces because it can be tailored to suit the space. However, it is obviously hard to take away when you move, and so it may not be the most economical option. One way around this is to create a cheap and basic fixed framework, perhaps using built-in shelves, and then subdivide the area with relatively inexpensive movable boxes.

freestanding storage

Sideboards, wardrobes, and trunks are just a few of the freestanding options. They often add decorative character to a room, and so make good focal points (although large and bulky examples can overwhelm smaller rooms). If you are the nomadic type, invest in the smaller items, such as chests of drawers or modular systems, as these are more likely to adapt to new surroundings.

storage: covering all the options

freestanding: reused shop cabinet

hooks and pegs A hook or peg is often all that you will need to turn dead space into useful storage. Attaching them to a cupboard door, for example, allows you to create a home for flat items such as saucepan lids. Hooks are

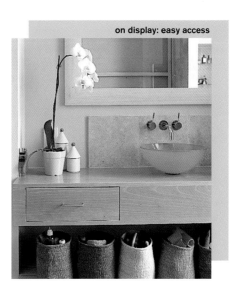

perfect wherever you need to keep objects close at hand, but off the floor and work surfaces.

modular storage

A modular system can consist simply of boxes stacked or fastened to the wall, or it can be a complex mix of storage, display areas, and work surfaces. Many systems can be added to over time, which is just as well, as the cost of putting together a tailor-made package

soon mounts up. Some are better designed than others – make sure that the one you choose allows you to store a variety of shapes and sizes.

on display As well as imposing order on open storage areas and allowing you to shift items easily from one place to another, boxes, baskets, and other smaller-size containers often form pleasing displays. When stacked, they can be used as temporary furniture, even screening.

Always clearly label the contents of any nontransparent examples.

shelving: freestanding

The simple answer to many a storage problem is provided by freestanding shelving. The most basic form consists of lengths of boards held in place and separated by bricks or boxes. However, systems that consist of shelves and uprights, with cross-braces for added stability, can easily be had for just a little more money. Look for one with a degree of adjustability. Screw units to the wall if there are children around.

shelving: wall-mounted

A loaded shelf seldom gets moved around, so it often makes sense to

fasten it permanently. Some hardware is suitable for a flush wall and some for an alcove. Fixed shelving also allows you to make a decorative feature out of your storage: more ornate brackets can be used, or the edge of the shelf given an unusual profile.

Adjustable wall-mounted shelving, on the other hand, is best for those areas where the stored items change regularly – in a walk-in wardrobe or cellar, for example. It's also useful if you are an inveterate rearranger of ornaments, books, and other displays. Almost all the systems available are based on a combination of uprights and brackets. It may also be possible to hang cabinets from the uprights to widen your options.

designing your own storage

Designing a tailor-made storage system isn't difficult or expensive. Just follow this simple guide:

1 First, get rid of those items that you no longer want or use, but have simply gotten used to having around. Do this regularly!

2 Activity will probably be concentrated in certain rooms. If you are fighting for space in these places, try to move little-used items, such as old books or special-occasion china, into less intensively used areas such as the hallway or basement. One of the golden rules of storage is that the more you use an item, the more accessible it needs to be.

3 Sort possessions according to type. Think about how you might store them so that it is easy to retrieve a single item and put it back when you have finished. T-shirts and sweaters, for example, are easiest to sort through when placed no more than three or four high on shelves, while cups can be put on shelves or hung from hooks.

4 Another golden rule of storage is that the smaller the item, the more compact its home needs to be. For example, subdivide kitchen cupboards with extra shelves so that ingredients and tableware can be arranged in neat rows rather than teetering piles. Think also about the weight of the items being stored: a row of books weighs more than a few clothes, and the shelf supporting them should be correspondingly stronger.

5 Some items will have specific requirements. Jackets can only be placed on hangers, and large suitcases are difficult to move in and out of tight spaces, while medicines and household cleaning supplies should be kept away from children and extreme temperatures.

6 Make sure that storage doesn't block your way or your view. Avoid placing it in front of heaters, outlets and other utilities. In smaller rooms, wall-mounted storage is good as it helps to keep the floor clear.

7 Always allow room for future acquisitions. It's also a good idea to build extra strength into a storage system, not only to make it last longer, but also to allow for future changes in use.

left **Tailor your storage to fit your possessions. Use the grids on pages 150–151 to design customized solutions.**

home fact file
doing it yourself

*Having decided on the "look" of a room
and the decorating projects that you will
undertake yourself, put plans into practice
with shopping lists of the tools and materials
required. When thinking about furniture,
consider storage, and use the space provided
to note how you will keep your belongings.
Grids provide you with the option of creating
customized designs for pieces such as
shelving and wardrobe divisions.*

shopping lists

costs   source

project:
_____

tools required:
_____
_____
_____
_____

materials required:
_____
_____
_____
_____

project:
_____

tools required:
_____
_____
_____
_____

materials required:
_____
_____
_____
_____

project:
_____

tools required:
_____
_____
_____
_____

materials required:
_____
_____
_____
_____

Create shopping lists and budgets for the decorating projects you are undertaking (your own or any of those from pages 116–139).

costs   source

project:

tools required:

materials required:

project:

tools required:

materials required:

project:

tools required:

materials required:

determining storage

hall
storage solution

- coats, umbrellas, etc.
- shoes
- keys
- other

living room

- books
- magazines and newspapers
- home entertainment equipment
- CDs, cassettes, etc.
- drinks and glassware
- other

kitchen

- fresh food
- packaged food
- crockery and glassware
- cutlery and cooking utensils
- tableware
- cookware
- tablecloths and napkins
- cookbooks
- shopping bags
- waste and recycling
- cleaning materials

study

- books and journals
- filing
- notepaper, envelopes, etc.
- pens, paper clips, etc.
- telephone directories
- computer disks and accessories
- other

bedroom

- spare bedding
- books and magazines
- home entertainment equipment

storage solution

▶ CDs, cassettes, etc.
▶ ornaments
▶ other

dressing area

▶ jackets and coats
▶ trousers
▶ skirts
▶ dresses
▶ shirts
▶ sweaters
▶ underwear
▶ sportswear
▶ T-shirts
▶ ties, belts, etc.
▶ scarves
▶ socks, tights, etc.
▶ shoes
▶ jewelry
▶ cosmetics
▶ other

bathroom

▶ medicines and toiletries
▶ towels, etc.
▶ cleaning materials
▶ other

miscellaneous

▶ laundry
▶ luggage
▶ tool box, ladder, etc.
▶ vacuum cleaner, broom, etc.
▶ ironing board and iron
▶ camera
▶ sports equipment
▶ bought-in-bulk items
▶ gardening equipment

design grids

fast
facelifts

easy, effective changes

above **This space is given a warm, exotic feel by putting up brightly colored drawings, a painted canvas hanging, and colored voile. Spindly accessories help to update the look.**

above right **Strings of lights may not be ultratasteful, but are a cheerful change from more standard bedroom lighting.**

There are plenty of times when completely redecorating a room is simply not an option; there may even be times when it's not particularly desirable. Much depends on whether you can live with the decor. If you strongly dislike the previous occupant's or landlord's taste in colors and patterns, your first step is going to have to be to cover it up as far as possible. Large sheets of fabric can be wrapped and tucked around furniture, and it may be possible to cover a large area of offensive carpet with a rug that is more to your tastes. The walls are

likely to be more of a challenge, although plastering them with pictures works well. Don't completely cover them with images unless you're sure you can live with full-on pattern. If you're not certain, some areas should be left plain, to provide visual relief. Alternatively, you could make a big and bold statement to create a focal point, and so help to distract the eye from any horrors that may be lurking elsewhere in the room.

Sometimes, updating just one element of a scheme makes a dramatic difference. To begin with, take a look at the windows:

Would a simpler and lighter curtain or blind treatment make the room feel fresher? Or, can you cozy it up with a layered look? If a space feels generally bland and lacking in color, try filtering the daylight through colored voiles or muslin to give the room's contents a subtle glow.

It's amazing how much cozier most rooms look when they are lit with light sources placed low down, rather than from above. Install extra lights in the kitchen, where work areas should be kept shadow-free, and in the bathroom, where your face needs to be evenly lit when you stand in front of the mirror. When a room works well on a practical level, its decorative shortcomings become less of an issue.

Once you are happy with the overall appearance of a room, try freshening it up with soft furnishings. Tired upholstered furniture can be smartened up with the help of a throw and one or two pillows in fashionable colors and textures. If you match these to the color of the walls, it will also help to blend a clunky piece of furniture into the background.

above **Fake flowers turn an expanse of dull blank wall into a colorful focal and talking point.**

RELATED PAGES

163 summer facelift

165 winter facelift

167 quick fix: party

customizing furniture

If you are finding it hard to track down attractive, well-priced furniture, why not try creating your own, by customizing junk shop items and hand-me-downs? You don't need any expert knowledge, although it helps to master a few basic techniques if you plan to do it on a regular basis. Just wander the aisles of your local home improvement store: you'll find they're packed with products and tools that make it easier than ever to clean up and decorate furniture. If you're not tempted by one of the many special paints or paint effects now available, look out for power tools that allow you to strip, sand and polish up the most awkward corners or intricate surfaces, and high-tech adhesives and fillers that will make short work of complex or tricky repairs.

Always make sure a piece of furniture is structurally sound before you start working

on it, and beware of damage to woven seat bases and backs and those with interior springs. Repairing these can cost a lot, as it usually involves sending for a professional.

Wood and metal furniture is especially easy to "do up." A wide variety of paints, stains, and dyes are available, and if a piece consists of flat surfaces, it can be livened up with pattern, applied freehand or using stencils. Flat surfaces can also be covered with other materials; for example, a kitchen table can be given a new lease on life either by gluing zinc sheeting to the top with a strong contact adhesive, or applying wipe-clean self-adhesive plastic. Even fabric can be used – this works best on simple, flat pieces that will not be subject to too much wear and tear.

You may only need to change or replace one or two parts to update a piece. A plain cabinet can be given character simply by changing the handles, and a new seat pad fabric may be all you need to smarten up some dining chairs. Alternatively, use a coffee table to display pictures, photographs, or fabrics by securing them under a top layer of tempered glass or clear acrylic. If you have this cut specially, always remember to ask for the edges to be polished, and then keep it in place with special washers or table corner protectors.

When you are feeling a bit more confident, try altering the basic shape and function of a simple piece. If you never use the dining table, for example, why not shorten

quick tips

▸ To add pattern to a plain surface, mask off selected areas and then paint around them. You could create masks from leaves for a natural feel or closely spaced pieces of cardboard to imitate a mosaic. Rubbing areas with wax, prior to painting, will produce a distressed finish.

▸ Spray paints give faster results and a more even finish, but use in well-ventilated areas and wear a face mask.

▸ Use fabric dyes to cheer up plain sheets or lengths of canvas before turning them into covers for sofas and armchairs.

▸ Large headscarves (or fabric remnants of a similar size) make great no-sew cushion covers. Simply place the cushion in the center of the fabric square, bring the corners of the fabric together, and secure by knotting or with a length of ribbon.

its legs to make a useful low table for use elsewhere? Or you could add more shelves to a cupboard, and thereby improve its storage capabilities.

If you have inherited some shabby and tasteless built-in cupboards along with your new home, you'll be glad to hear that they are just as easy to transform. Even melamine-faced doors can be painted, as long as they are first primed with a suitable product. Once the paint has dried, give the doors a new set of handles to complete the look. Alternatively, you could simply remove the doors, and replace them with blinds or curtains.

The easiest way to update a piece of upholstered furniture is to cover it up, either with a loose cover (these can be specially made or bought off-the-shelf) or by simply wrapping it in a sheet of fabric.

RELATED PAGES

60 preparing woodwork

64 preparing metalwork

customizing fabrics

When you are working with fabric, you should never skimp on quantity. Curtains need fullness if they are to frame the window properly and do a good job of keeping out light and drafts. Likewise, pillows look more inviting if they are generously sized and trimmed.

Certain fabrics are also easier to customize. Cotton comes at the top of the list, because it's cheap, absorbs color well, and is easy to work with. It is also available in a range of weights, from floaty muslin to stiff, virtually indestructible canvas. Alternatively, take a look at lining materials, felt, silk, and knitted fabrics.

One of the simplest and most straightforward options is to change the color of your fabric using dyes.

above **Soft furnishings can add the final touch to a room. A fabric that doesn't fray easily, such as felt, is ideal for making simple appliquéd pillows.**

Fabrics soften, warm up, and "finish off" a room scheme, which makes them pretty well indispensable. Unfortunately, they can also make a big hole in your budget, unless you are prepared to skimp on quantities, or live with dated and dull designs. With a touch of imagination, however, simple fabrics and soft furnishings can be customized to create a more exciting and "pulled together" look. They can be dyed, printed, painted on, and trimmed with a wide variety of materials. In the case of curtains, they can also be dressed up with decorative rods, tiebacks, and other fittings.

These are now easier to use, and more likely to give even results, than ever. Some of the latest formulations can also be used in a washing machine without risk of staining. Use them just as they are, or combine them with a resist technique, such as tie-dye or batik, to create patterns on the fabric. When you want to create localized areas of pattern, or a bold motif, you will need to paint or print them on. Lay the fabric perfectly flat in order to draw on the design (remember to protect the surface underneath). It's always a good idea to do a test run on a reasonably sized remnant, to check that the scale and repeat of the design matches your expectations. Fabric marker pens, as well as paints, are widely available. The former are ideal for drawing lines or fine detail.

If you simply want to liven up basic soft furnishings, you'll find a dazzling variety of trimmings, made from both traditional and more unconventional materials, in any good notions store or department store. For a neat and simple finish, look out for braids, ribbons, rope edgings, and tapes. If you favor a more

theatrical look, you won't be able to resist the bobble fringes, tassels, sequins, and beads available. You don't have to use specially made trimmings either; a contrasting band of fabric makes a smart and unfussy edging for curtains, blinds, and pillows. Or you could be more whimsical, and sew on shells, seed pods, or dried flowers.

above left **Create soft furnishings with a bold, graphic feel simply by joining fabric panels of different colors together.**

above **Cheer up plain curtains with quirky tie-backs, and transform dull sofas with pillows made from sparkly fabrics.**

display

Whatever you plan to display, you must consider its scale, the way it is to be lit, and its placement in relation to other items. The most stunning pieces will look insignificant if they are simply scattered around at random. Group objects thematically, and try to ensure that they look as though they belong in a particular location.

Of course, the location you choose should be fit for its purpose. Placing delicate glassware where it could be knocked over easily, for example, will simply make you feel uneasy, and there is nothing attractive about flimsy shelves that are about to give way under the weight of massed books.

If you want to highlight a single object, it needs to contrast strongly with its surroundings. You can do this by keeping the area around it clear, or by teaming it with items that are its opposite in terms of scale, texture, and color. For example, a small picture will instantly engage your attention if it is surrounded by a blank wall, as long as it is placed at a convenient height and is clearly lit. Or you could team a tall vase with low dishes in order to exaggerate the height of the former.

Once you have seen how much displays can improve the look and mood of a room, you may not want to stop. There is always

above Sticking to one or two colors is a great way to give a varied grouping of objects a coherent feel.

Pictures, books, china, plants, and other treasures do more than any other element of a decorative scheme to create life and warmth. Displaying them reveals your tastes and interests – they truly make the room your own. And as they can be introduced and moved around easily, they really can be used to transform or to update a space instantly.

above **A simple peg rack gives a display of bags a casual and witty feel, while ensuring that they are safely stored and clearly seen.**

left **This culinary variation on a bead curtain – made of hooks and chains – makes an exciting, amusing, and, importantly, practical display.**

the temptation to add just one more picture to that striking grouping on the wall, or to shift stuff around so that you can squeeze one more item on to the tabletop or mantelpiece. Beware though, for the line that divides collections and clutter is easily crossed. If you find yourself edging around a display, or having to move items out of the way before you can put down a cup or newspaper, you have definitely gone too far, and the time has come to rehouse your collection or do some serious weeding out.

RELATED PAGES

92 personalizing the space

summer facelift

- ▸ Help to bounce daylight around a room.
- ▸ Provide a cool and refreshing backdrop.
- ▸ Are easy to create using liming paste, bleach, or a paint colorwash.

whitened floors

summer fabrics

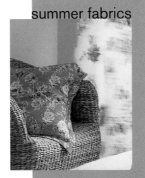

- ▸ Choose sheers (voile, muslin, or lace) or natural fabrics (linen, calico, or cotton) in fresh colors for window treatments and soft furnishings. Tough cotton canvas and calico make great loose covers.
- ▸ Stick to simple patterns such as florals or stripes.

- ▸ Plants provide a link with the outside. Twigs and seed pods create evocative still-life arrangements.
- ▸ Grouped vases of scented flowers help to freshen stale summer air.

greenery

outdoor furniture

- ▸ Lightweight and folding – providing flexibility and creating a relaxed feel.
- ▸ Like other outdoor materials and furnishings, it helps to bring a sense of the outside indoors.

As the temperature rises, rooms start to fill with warm sunshine and it seems to stay light outdoors until bedtime. It feels right to look outwards again, and to blur the distinctions between the outdoors and inside.

To begin with, let the daylight in. Dress your windows with light and translucent materials such as cottons and voiles, and bounce the light into the room with the help of a pale floor or light-colored furnishings. Think about paring down the contents of the room too. If you have fireside accessories or wintry soft furnishings, put them away until the weather changes again.

This airier feel can be complemented by colors, materials, and accessories that echo those found outdoors or in the garden. Add a touch of fresh green, or the colors of summer flowers such as rosy pinks and blue delphiniums.

The worn and patinated surfaces of materials such as galvanized or enameled metal, teak, and terra-cotta will instantly loosen a room up, especially if introduced in the form of garden pots and furniture.

far left **Accessorizing a neutral space with sunny yellows and greens helps to bring the outdoors in, while pretty furnishings, such as the tablecloth, stop the room from looking too stark.**

winter facelift

rich fabrics

- Suggest warmth through earthy colors and strokable textures.
- Trimmings add luxury, and ethnic-inspired patterns conjure up the exotic.

color

- Orangey reds, gold and black make a space womblike and are magical lit by candlelight at night.
- Combine with cream or stone colors if the room is used during the day.

accessories

- Handcrafted items in rich colors add weight and character.
- Add one or two pale elements to provide visual relief.

sparkle

- Lanterns and candles flicker like fire.
- Metallic surfaces hold and reflect the light.
- Use dimmers on light switches to create a softer, more intimate mood.

The arrival of colder weather often kindles a strong desire to snuggle up indoors and stay put. If this sounds like your idea of heaven, make the experience pure bliss with rooms that feel as cozy and as welcoming as possible. This doesn't have to mean redecorating, although painting the walls a warmer shade can make a huge difference. Instead, think about adding materials and accessories that feel warm to the touch, such as wood or strokable velvet and wool. Another great trick is to use materials and finishes that have a sunny or fiery quality, such as gilt and brass. Of course, you can also add real fire in the form of candles and other types of lighting.

Surprisingly small amounts of such materials are needed: placing a single red object, such as a table lamp or pillow, in a neutral space makes a discernible difference. If you like your decor to be bold, however, go for riotous mixes of color and pattern.

Of course, your home should be physically warm too. Don't forget to weatherproof doors and windows, and make sure the heating is working efficiently.

far left **The colors and crafts of Latin America, instantly evoking the warmth of that region's climate and culture, are exploited to the full in this dramatic and glamorous dining room.**